The Fifty Greatest JAZZ Piano Players of All Time

The Fifty Greatest JAZZ Piano Players of All Time

Ranking, Analysis & Photos By Gene Rizzo

HAL•LEONARD®
CORPORATION
7777 W. BLUEMOUND RD. P.O. BOX 13819 MILWAUKEE, WI 53213

Cover Photo Credits: L–R: Thelonius Monk, Chick Corea, Bill Evans, Cedar Walton courtesy Lee Tanner/Jazz Image. Photo of Count Basie courtesy Frank Driggs Collection.

ISBN 0-634-07416-4

Published by Hal Leonard Corporation
7777 W. Bluemound Road
P.O. Box 13819
Milwaukee, WI 53213

In Australia Contact:
Hal Leonard Australia Pty. Ltd.
4 Lentara Court
Cheltenham, Victoria, 3192 Australia
Email: ausadmin@halleonard.com

Hal Leonard books are available at your local bookstore, or you may order through Music Dispatch at 1-800-637-2852 or www.musicdispatch.com.

Library of Congress Cataloging-in-Publication Data

Rizzo, Gene.
   The fifty greatest jazz piano players of all time : ranking, analysis & photos / by Gene Rizzo.--1st ed.
      p. cm.
   ISBN 0-634-07416-4
   1. Pianists--Biography. 2. Jazz musicians--Biography. I. Title.
ML397.R59 2005
786.2'165'0922--dc22
                        2005003778

Printed in the U.S.A.

First Edition

Visit Hal Leonard online at
www.halleonard.com

Dedication

For all "ticklers'" mothers—
But especially for Mrs. Ida Perry Rizzo

Foreword

"It is a singular thing," Nathaniel Hawthorne wrote, "that, at the distance, say, of five feet, the work of the greatest dunce looks just as well as that of the greatest genius—that little space being all the distance between genius and stupidity." To close the gap of "that little space," for the selection of 50 of jazz's greatest pianists, the Hal Leonard Corporation has impaneled not only its best jazz minds, and those of top educators and musicians, but the author's humble services as well. Names that do not appear among the chosen 50 were not dismissed as dunces (Hawthorne exaggerates, of course, to make his point), nor is genius always to be inferred by the names that do appear. Genius is no more common in jazz than it is in other art forms. Choices were made on the basis of creativity, degree of influence, and command of the instrument, with a particular emphasis on artists in whom those factors converge. The results are racially and demographically diverse. With apologies to the women's movement, there is only one female entry. Perhaps another survey of this kind in the next decade will reflect the swiftly vanishing social conventions that once restricted jazz careers for women.

The artists have been accorded brief bios, stylistic analyses, and a survey of their most representative recordings. Our electoral body is fully aware that the reader may not always agree with the rating order, or the opinions expressed herein. Hawthorne notwithstanding, the quantification of talent is tricky business—even at point-blank range.

—Gene Rizzo

Contents

50 The Top Fifty

Photo: Frank Driggs Collection

Oscar Peterson
(1 9 2 5 -   )

Oscar Peterson found fame after a comparatively short sideman apprenticeship—a privilege rarely afforded players of those instruments lacking the self-contained capacities of the piano. His monumental technique, sandblasted clean of any imperfections, dynamic originality, and contagiously swinging beat, were already in full bloom for his Carnegie Hall debut in 1949. The assets bode well for the then 24-year-old Canadian's future. Clearly, he had no need for the jazz witness-protection program into which so many hopeful foreign-born pianists vanished, particularly in the 1950s. (Does anyone remember Jutta Hipp, Bernard Peiffer, or Friedrich Gulda?) The winner of thirteen consecutive *Downbeat* polls from 1950 to 1963, *Playboy* magazine's Musicians' Musician ten times over, the honoree of ten doctorates, the conferee of the Medal of Service of the Order of Canada (1973), and the Companion of the Order of Canada (1983), Peterson has cast a giant shadow on jazz piano tradition for more than half a century.

Peterson was born the fourth of five children in Montreal, Quebec. His father, a railroad porter from the Virgin Islands and a passionate musical amateur, originally assigned his five-year-old son the role of trumpeter in the family band. The boy doubled on trumpet and piano until a bout with tuberculosis, contracted at seven, ended his playing aspirations on a wind instrument. Concentrating exclusively on the piano, he studied first with his older sister, Daisy, and thereafter with Paul de Marky, a concert pianist trained by a student of Franz Liszt. The rigors of classical training suited Peterson's determined, competitive nature. He practiced as much as twelve hours a day. While attending Montreal High School, he worked in a band led by the brother of his schoolmate, Maynard Ferguson. In 1944, he joined the Johnny Holmes dance orchestra.

After hearing him in the Alberta Lounge (1949), jazz impresario Norman Granz convinced Peterson to try his luck in the States. The pianist parlayed his initial success at Carnegie Hall into becoming a fixture of Granz's Jazz at the Philharmonic concerts for a time, but his trio's Nat "King" Cole-inspired instrumentation (piano, bass, guitar) ultimately became a separate global attraction under Granz's personal management. Ray Brown, the group's bassist, stayed on when guitarist Herb Ellis, who was replaced by drummer Ed Thigpen, left in 1959. As the years went on, other teammates included bassists Sam Jones, Niels-Henning Ørsted Pedersen, and drummers Martin Drew and Bobby Durham. A paralyzing stroke in 1993 (from which he recovered after two grueling years of physical therapy) temporarily halted the Peterson juggernaut. His former glory as the supreme master of jazz piano was only slightly tarnished when he returned to active playing.

Peterson references the styles of Art Tatum, Teddy Wilson, Nat "King" Cole, and George Shearing in a very personal way. He cannot be mistaken for anyone else. By the late '60s, his ballad playing began to take on the evocative sheen of Bill Evans's work. The influence did not extend, however, to Evans's trailblazing explorations of implied time and equally shared trio interplay. In an Oscar Peterson trio, emphatic, foot-stomping time is never absent, and the piano still does most of the heavy lifting (*History of an Artist*, Pablo Records, 1972–74). The septuagenarian's recent recordings still offer extraordinary moments (*The Very Tall Band Live at the Blue Note*, Telarc Records, 1998).

Photo: Lee Tanner/Jazz Image

Bill Evans

(1 9 2 9 - 1 9 8 0)

Of all the analogies drawn between jazz pianists and classical composers (i.e., Oscar Peterson and Liszt, Teddy Wilson and Mozart), the common pairing of Bill Evans with Chopin is the least specious. Evans's signature qualities—a penchant for understatement, a singing tone, an intricate harmonic imagination—are indeed requisites for a convincing Chopin interpretation. The twain also meet as the most original and influential figures of their respective times; each quietly rebelled against a prevailing trend—Chopin protesting mere sideshow acrobatics at the piano and Evans refusing to pander to the hard bop school of the 1950s and '60s. The results set trends of their own. Chopinistas were once as plentiful as Evansistas are now. Sadly, we will only know the great Slavic composer's playing through his channeler/spokesmen, but his jazz counterpart can be heard on a cornucopia of recordings for no more than the price of a whistling teakettle.

Born in Plainfield, New Jersey, Evans's piano lessons began at the age of six. At seven, he took up the violin. He later studied the flute and piccolo under the guidance of his high school music teacher, but the piano remained his first love. After graduating from Southeastern Louisiana College with bachelor of music and bachelor of music education degrees, he served in the Army (1951–54). Stationed at Fort Sheridan near Chicago, he became a student of George Russell, whose modal-based concepts were to inform Evans's playing from then on. While working with Tony Scott in New York, Evans made his first recordings as a leader (*New Jazz Conceptions*, Riverside Records, 1956). The album set the then twenty-something jazz pianist apart from his funk-addled contemporaries. As hard bop evolved, Evans's reflective style began to lure many converts. He spent most of 1958 with the Miles Davis Sextet. No longer a Davis sideman, in 1959 he guested on the trumpet icon's visionary *Kind of Blue* album for which he is given too little credit as co-arranger and composer.

A high-profile, and much imitated trio leader for the remaining years of his life, Evans encouraged his sidemen to redefine the traditional roles of bass and drums in piano trios. His groups spawned new frontiers of sensitive interaction and time delineation among the players. Bassists Scott La Faro and Eddie Gomez, and drummers Paul Motian and Eliot Zigmund, are alumni of these groundbreaking efforts.

Evans could also be perfectly autonomous as he proved on *Conversations with Myself* (Verve Records, 1963) and *Further Conversations with Myself* (Verve Records, 1967). Both sessions borrow from Lennie Tristano's experiments of the mid '50s, wherein the artist dialogues against himself via multi-track recording technology.

As a composer, Evans's "Waltz for Debby" has an enormous cachet among musicians and fans. His brooding "Peace Piece" captures the fervent commitment of a foxhole prayer.

A lifelong activist on behalf of Bud Powell ("His insight and talent," Evans wrote, "were unmatched in hard-core, true jazz"), he was nonetheless never overtly influenced by him. Something of that older master's agitated harmonic rhythm is retained, however, and suffused with soft, dense Ravelian chords. Linkage to the styles of Nat "King" Cole, Al Haig, and Lennie Tristano is clear in Evans's nimble, yet lyrical, passagework. He rarely unleashed his virtuosity for its own sake, but an Evans ballad coda can erupt like a sudden summer storm. His death after decades of drug abuse is an inconsolable loss.

Photo: Frank Driggs Collection

3 Bud Powell

(1924 - 1966)

Bud Powell revolutionized jazz piano technique. The piano did not become an

integral force in bebop until Powell eliminated some of the instrument's previous

stylistic baggage. He replaced the oompah of stride jazz with spare voicings on

accented upbeats, exchanged niceties of tone and articulation for driving swing,

shunned the comfort zones of clichés within easy reach, and generally bypassed

the Earl Hines, Fats Waller, and Art Tatum traditions which preceded him. Inspired

by his idol, Charlie Parker, Powell's conception is more horn-like than pianistic—

he did not play piano so much as he *blew* it.

Powell was born in New York City. The son of an amateur stride pianist, he was classically trained from the age of five. In the early '40s, barely out of his teens, he began to take part in the experimental jam sessions at Minton's Playhouse. His early influences were Tatum and Teddy Wilson—suitable idols for a young pianist with take-no-prisoners chops. The innovative company he was keeping at Minton's (Thelonious Monk, Parker and Dizzy Gillespie—the de facto brain trust of the bop movement) pointed him in other directions. After working as a sideman with Fats Navarro, Sonny Stitt, and J.J. Johnson, his destiny as a pioneer was fulfilled.

His first recordings as a leader, a trio session for Roost in '47, followed by a quintet date in '49, and more trio outings for Blue Note in '51, had the effect of a cold shower on jazz pianists of every persuasion. All are available on *Bud Powell: The Complete Blue Note and Roost Recordings*, a five-CD set on Blue Note, which includes a few of his well crafted contributions as a composer: "Glass Enclosure," "Dance of the Infidels," and "Un Poco Loco."

A new and highly influential paradigm had arrived. Ray Bryant noted, "He [Powell] influenced everyone after him, and those before him modified their style." Powell's genius was in full bloom, replete with dramatic intros and restless harmonic rhythm. Intensely driven chromatic lines poured out of him like hot streams of lava. The effect was electric, super-charged. Powell never phoned in a performance. Even his ballads were only relatively serene; Tatum-esque, they suggest how Tatum might have sounded at slower tempos if he had invested more emotional capital in his approach.

These were the years before Powell's dependency on drugs and alcohol overtook him—before cracks began to appear in his psyche and he sank into madness. His later recordings are erratic, reflecting his personal problems here, and the compelling artist-of-old there. He reached a certain amount of celebrity but never enjoyed more than modest financial success. Although Paris received him well during the years he lived there (1959–64), his repatriation to the USA was less than spectacular. He died in New York City.

Powell's style, once so controversial, is the template for what decades of widespread imitation have reduced to common coin. It is hard to imagine what jazz piano would sound like if he had left it the way he found it.

Photo: Frank Driggs Collection

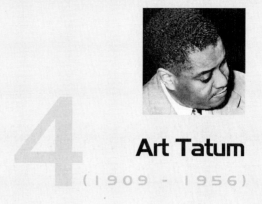

4 Art Tatum
(1909 - 1956)

Art Tatum scared the bejesus out of piano players. His virtuosity and harmonic daring could be truly hair-raising. After hearing Tatum for the first time, Oscar Peterson had crying fits at night and didn't touch the piano for two months. Organist Wild Bill Davis and guitarist Les Paul completely scrubbed their early pianistic aspirations after their encounters with the colossus. Tatum rarely inspired piano vocations as Fats Waller, Teddy Wilson, and Bud Powell did; musicians were more likely to study the instrument in spite of him, rather than because of him.

Born nearly blind in Toledo, Ohio, Tatum gave a glimpse of his future impact on an unsuspecting world by pecking out hymns on the family piano at the age of three. He later excelled at learning thorough-composed pieces, in Braille, at the Toledo School of Music, where a strong bond was formed between him and his visually impaired teacher, Overton G. Rainey. Rainey tried to prepare his brilliant student for a career as a concert pianist. The prospect was unrealistic for a black artist at the time, and was further sabotaged by Tatum's attraction to the Harlem stride style of Fats Waller. In any case, the association with Rainey nurtured an already astonishing technique. (Ironically, Tatum, a born concert artist as few have never been, played in only a handful of concert halls during his lifetime.)

By his mid-teens, Tatum was working in the local bands of Speed Webb and Milt Senior. At eighteen, he was given his own regularly scheduled radio show on WSPD in Toledo. He seized a window of opportunity when singer Adelaide Hall took him to New York as her accompanist in 1932. There Tatum gave full rein to the competitive nature he hid under a benevolent veneer, and drew blood night-ly from many a super-strider in Harlem's notorious cutting contests. When Tatum was spotted in the audience of a Fats Waller engagement, Waller famously remarked, "God is in the house"—an acknowledgement of an old dueling scar.

Tatum's fame spread, prompting his first recordings (*Art Tatum*, Classics Records (France), 1932–34), and after-hours jobs on 52nd Street. In 1934, he left New

York for a long hiatus, working in radio and clubs in the Midwest and California. Returning to the Big Apple in '38, he played mostly solo dates until he formed a trio based on the Nat "King" Cole model of piano, bass, and guitar ('43). In spite of his remarkable colleagues—Tiny Grimes on guitar and Slam Stewart on bass—Tatum soon tired of the brakes the group put on his fertile imagination. The trio disbanded after little more than a year.

Solo playing was always Tatum's medium of choice. Unfettered by the limits of a team effort, he could expand the dollhouse scale of a simple pop song into a towering skyscraper. Many of his harmonic and melodic ideas were adopted by Teddy Wilson, Bud Powell (thereby presaging bebop piano), and Oscar Peterson. Peterson became Tatum's de facto protégé and singularly mastered his mentor's ability to execute avalanches of richly layered chords and dizzying passagework without crossing pianistic boundaries into a bogus orchestral style.

Tatum continued to evolve as an inimitable lone wolf through the '40s and the better part of the '50s. The recordings of his final years include a landmark series of extended solos produced by Norman Granz (*The Complete Pablo Solo Masterpieces*, Pablo Records, 1953–55, a seven-CD set). A quartet session with tenor sax giant Ben Webster (*Tatum Group Masterpieces Vol. 8*, Pablo Records, 1956), recorded within weeks of the pianist's death from uremia, is a brilliant, but sad farewell. If Tatum wasn't a genius, he was at least within striking distance of being one.

Photo: Alan Nahigian

5 Monty Alexander
(1 9 4 4 -   )

Blessed with a swinging style that can energize the most slogging tempo, Monty

Alexander has morphed from the leader a popular Jamaican band to rising jazz star

to world-class concert and recording artist. His sunny, high-spirited playing mirrors

his West Indian roots. Original without being arcane, he retains only a few small

souvenirs from the weaponry he seized in raids on Nat "King" Cole and Oscar

Peterson's war chests. Alexander is a member of a vanishing breed in jazz piano—

the unabashed romantic. He may be the most in-your-face melodist since Erroll

Garner. He also has technique to burn, and makes excellent use of the surplus.

Alexander was born in Kingston, Jamaica. His piano studies stretched from the ages of six to fourteen. The live appearances of Louis Armstrong and Nat "King" Cole that he attended at the Carib Theater deeply influenced his musical development. By his mid-teens, he was sitting in with prominent local musicians. Recordings by his reggae group, Monty and the Cyclones, scored high on the Jamaican pop charts from 1958 to 1960.

In 1961, Alexander moved to Miami, Florida, where he played with Art Mooney's orchestra and later freelanced as a solo pianist. After hearing him in a nightclub, Jilly Rizzo, of Frank Sinatra fame, invited the young musician to work in his eponymously named New York bistro. The offer came to nothing, but was extended again in the summer of 1963 when Rizzo heard Alexander in Las Vegas, Nevada. Endorsed by Ol' Blue Eyes himself, who was present on both occasions, the proposition was followed through.

Jilly's, a west side watering hole for Sinatra and other celebrities in music and entertainment, was Alexander's steady gig until 1967 when he joined Milt Jackson. He formed his own trio in 1974. In the mid '80s, he became a member of Triple Threat, an empathetic supertrio that included Ray Brown and Herb Ellis. After the demise of Triple Threat, the pianist participated in several tributes to jazz legends: as sideman on the soundtrack of *Bird*, Clint Eastwood's film bio of Charlie

Parker (1988); as assistant on Natalie Cole's seven-time Grammy Award winning album in memory of her father, Nat "King" Cole, *Unforgettable*, 1991); as a featured artist for a celebration of Erroll Garner at Carnegie Hall (1993); and as accompanist for operatic soprano Barbara Hendricks's salute to Duke Ellington at Montreux (1994 and '95). He continues to perform with his trio, a favorite group on the festival circuit.

A pair of Alexander's recordings from the '90s is worthy of special note. In keeping with his heritage, *Yard Movement* (Concord, 1995) offers steel drums and backbeat guitar work in a refreshing confluence of pan-Caribbean and jazz ideas. On *Echoes of Jilly's* (Concord, 1997), he cleaves to some choice Nat "King" Cole-ish licks; likewise, there is enough of the flavor of Oscar Peterson's style to justify Peterson's reference in his autobiography to Alexander as "my little West Indian counterpart." Alexander's runs, however—the sudden and dazzling aural equivalent of a magician fanning out a deck of cards—are sheathed in a very personal lyricism. Ditto his ear for lush, island harmony. With more than fifty albums to his credit over the years, and a busy schedule of live engagements, the pianist's beat goes on.

Photo: Alan Nahigian

6 Benny Green

(1963 -   )

Benny Green's accomplishments belie his years. His swift transformation from novice to master has been duly noted in the jazz press. Too little attention has been given, however, to the equally noteworthy reverence his playing has shown for the older traditions of the music. Precocious talent is not rare in jazz. Fats Waller, Earl Hines, Art Tatum, Teddy Wilson, and Bud Powell—members of what Oscar Peterson likes to call the "central dynasty of [jazz] piano"—were all young guns when they made their impressive debuts. The trick is to sustain interest after your fifteen minutes are up. Given the stylistic upheavals in jazz since Green's birth, he has made a lasting impression with his deep commitment to the blues, and a capacity to swing, which artists many years, even decades, his senior might envy.

The son of a tenor saxophonist, Green was born in New York City and raised in Berkeley, California. Classically trained from age seven, he began more jazz-oriented studies at nine with several teachers. Playing in the Berkeley High School band confirmed his musical vocation. He worked with Joe Henderson, Woody Shaw, and Eddie Henderson in San Francisco before the Green family moved back to New York City in 1982. Still eager to study, Green came under the tutelage of Walter Bishop, Jr., Walter Davis, Jr., and Larry Willis. Most of the remaining years of the '80s were spent in two important finishing schools for young jazz talent— vocalist Betty Carter's trio (1983–87), and Art Blakey's Jazz Messengers (1987–89). He joined Freddie Hubbard in '89, and left to form his own trio in '92. In 1993, Green was Oscar Peterson's personal choice for the first-place winner of the coveted Glenn Gould Protégé Prize.

Green has led one of the more listener-friendly piano trios of his generation (*Greens: The Benny Green Trio*, Blue Note Records, 1991). He is clearly aware of Bill Evans's innovations, which allow the rhythm section to provide more than just windshield-wiper timekeeping, but draws the line where Evans almost relinquished the role of the piano as the dominant instrument. In Green's high-concept arrangements of standards and original compositions (he is a standout tunesmith), the bass and drums are given intriguing parts to play, yet there is no doubt that the leader is point man in the presentation. Tommy Flanagan's last trios were similarly cast; their provenance, however, is closer to the Evans model. All the aforementioned have rescued the acoustic piano trio from obsolescence at a time when near-sensory modal vampers in three-way units of the bland-leading-the-bland roam the earth.

Green has evolved from a compendium of the styles of his forebears (particularly Horace Silver, Oscar Peterson, McCoy Tyner, and Herbie Hancock) into an artist with maverick tendencies of his own. On *These Are Soulful Days* (Blue Note, 1999), he is consistently finding fresh applications for his blues-laced harmony and authoritative single-note lines. Young creative artists like Green bode well for the future of jazz.

Photo: Redferns Music Picture Library

7 André Previn

(1929 -   )

André Previn approaches the repertoires of classical music and jazz with equal reverence and confidence. There is a revealing moment in the videotaped recording session *Kiri Te Kanawa* and *André Previn: Together on Broadway*. While the camera pans the control booth at the Sony studio in New York, the pianist muses on the soundtrack, for the benefit of the viewer, on the jitters of recording: "I don't think you say [to yourself], 'I don't have to be nervous about this—it's only Jerome Kern.'"

Previn was born in Berlin, Germany. Although a budding virtuoso by his preteens, he was cast out of the Berlin Conservatory in 1938 because he was a Jew. On the advice of an uncle, a film cutter at MGM, the Previn family fled from Nazi persecution to Los Angeles. At sixteen, Previn's keen study of the recordings of Art Tatum and Fats Waller led to his substituting on a film track for Jose Iturbi in a scene requiring a jazz solo that Iturbi couldn't play. The precocious youngster's composing and orchestrating skills were also called upon at MGM where he earned Academy Awards for scoring *Gigi* (1958), *Porgy and Bess* (1959), and *My Fair Lady* (1964).

Previn's grueling work schedule at the studio never threatened his interest in jazz. Together with drummer Shelly Manne (a personal friend for many years) and bassist Leroy Vinnegar, he recorded *My Fair Lady*—one of the best-selling jazz LPs of all time. This was followed by stylishly hip renderings of other Broadway musicals such as *Pal Joey*, *Bells Are Ringing*, *Gigi*, and *West Side Story*.

Although he left Hollywood in the mid '60s, launching a successful career as a conductor and composer for the concert stage, Previn still continues his jazz activities whenever possible on recordings and in live appearances.

Previn's playing is marked by virtuoso brilliance, razor-clear articulation, and harmonic practices inspired by 20th-century symphonic composers like Ravel and Prokofiev. Also, the West Coast pianists Russ Freeman, Carl Perkins, and Pete Jolly did not escape

Previn's attention during his Hollywood years; he has filtered something of their witty, swaggering essence through his own unique sensibilities. Previn's famous "Like Young," an infectiously funky little piece, demonstrates his remarkable affinity for the blues; indeed, there is a blues subtext in much of his playing. For all of these diverse elements, his style is personal and immediately recognizable.

Photo: Lee Tanner/Jazz Image

8 Tommy Flanagan
(1930 - 2001)

Tommy Flanagan's ultimate success as a soloist was delayed by the accumulation

of one of the most enviable accompanist résumés this side of Jimmy Rowles. An

émigré from Detroit to New York City in 1956, Flanagan was barely settled in his

Manhattan digs when he made his recording debut as a sideman with a posse of

fellow ex-Detroiters. Within a few days, he subbed for an ailing Bud Powell at

Birdland—a rare solo opportunity for him at the time. A sideman again, he partic-

ipated on two milestone recordings: *Saxophone Colossus* with Sonny Rollins

(Original Jazz Classics, 1956), and *Giant Steps* with John Coltrane (Atlantic, 1959).

By 1960, when Flanagan placed fifth on piano in the *Downbeat* International Critics' Poll, there were few major East Coast jazz artists who had not called upon his supporting services at one time or another. He shared stages with Ella Fitzgerald and Tony Bennett throughout the '60s and early '70s. Subordinate activities dominated his work schedule until the mid '70s when determined record producers, concert promoters, and club owners placed him in the limelight he continued to enjoy for the remaining years of his career.

Flanagan started on clarinet at six years of age, and switched to piano at ten. Some of his first jobs as a fifteen-year-old professional were played with tenor saxophonist Dexter Gordon. Later, as house pianist at such Detroit watering holes as the Blue Bird Inn and the Twenty Grand, Flanagan formed many strong artistic and personal ties with other musicians; a trend which continued in New York long after the great Motor City jazz exodus of the '50s. His first recording and other session reunions in the Big Apple with "home boy" confreres Hank and Elvin Jones and Kenny Burrell have produced some fine, high-spirited music.

Flanagan's horn-like style confirms his charter membership in the Detroit "school." His long, serpentine lines echo Bud Powell's paraphrasings of Charlie Parker. Flanagan's driving ideas at middle- and up-tempos belie his considerable resources as a ballad player. Lovers of sunsets and dinners by candlelight will appreciate his exquisite, dream-weaver reading of Horace Silver's "Peace" on *Something Borrowed, Something Blue* (Original Jazz Classics, 1978).

Flanagan is often compared with Hank Jones. While both reject the percussive, snowshoe-on-each-hand clangor that passes for creativity in some quarters, each arrives at compelling results in his own way. Flanagan uses slight pauses and unexpected accents in his lines to suggest a one-handed, two-part invention. His left hand calls little attention to itself, but neatly outlines the harmony. Jones traffics in the seamless *legato* line and a more active left hand. The two masters can be heard in a friendly face-off on *Tommy Flanagan and Hank Jones* (Original Jazz Classics, 1992).

Since the death of Bill Evans in 1980, Flanagan quietly assumed the stewardship of Evans's conception of the piano trio that replaced the traditional piano-soloist-with-rhythm-accompaniment paradigm with more equitable, three-way improvisation. Flanagan's trios increasingly emphasized implied, rather than explicit, timekeeping and overall interdependence between the players.

Photo: Frank Driggs Collection

George Shearing

(1 9 1 9 -   )

Congenitally blind, George Shearing was born the youngest of seven children in

Battersea, London. At the age of three, he could be found at the piano pecking

out tunes he'd heard on the family's crystal set. His handicap and precocious tal-

ent led to specialized education, but the study of classical piano and theory (ages

12–16 at the Linden Lodge School for the Blind) constitutes his only formal train-

ing in music. He rejected several university scholarship opportunities, opting for

the immediate earnings of working professionally. Soon a career that began in

neighborhood pubs expanded to recordings, engagements in top London supper

clubs, and guest spots on BBC radio.

During the war, Shearing met and impressed Fats Waller, Glenn Miller, and Coleman Hawkins while they were touring England. Each assured him of great success in the USA. In 1947, the future composer of "Lullaby of Birdland" finally crossed the Atlantic bound for New York, where he began to attract attention in the creative ferment of 52nd Street.

In '49, Shearing formed his famous quintet—a unique blend at the time of piano, vibes, guitar, bass, and drums. It became one of jazz's biggest attractions. The quintet's tight arrangements were based on the locked-hands style of Lionel Hampton's pianist, Milt Buckner. Its formula, easily atomized, but less easily executed at fast tempos, featured the piano voiced in four-part chords. The right hand's top, or melody voice, was doubled by the left hand within an octave. The vibes played in unison with the upper melody, the guitar with the lower.

After disbanding the quintet in '78, Shearing reduced his surroundings to a piano/bass duo. Qualities came to light which had previously been hidden under the guise of a kinder, gentler interpretation of the Bud Powell tradition—exemplary technique; a flair for richly layered, extended improvisation; a wit and verve as inseparable as Smith & Wesson. A master ballad player (like Tatum, one of his early idols), he is only a cat's whisker away from the melody even in his most florid passagework. Shearing's elegiac tone, however, is closer to that of Hank Jones—a peer for whom he has always expressed open admiration.

The personable Brit's most unique asset is his harmonic sense. Guided by an impeccable ear for voice leading, he freely moves inversionless five- and six-part chords without repeating notes. The effect is similar to the scaffolding of a Bach chorale; each "voice" is a singable, independent entity.

Shearing is well recorded. A highly selective discography should include *Velvet Carpet*, *Satin Affair*, *Latin Escapade* (all with the quintet, on Capitol Records), *Blues Alley Jazz*, *On a Clear Day*, and *Live at the Carlyle* (all in the piano/bass duo context, on Concord). His four albums with singer Mel Tormé (Concord) are object lessons in accompaniment.

Photo: Lee Tanner/Jazz Image

10 Red Garland
(1923 - 1984)

Listening to Red Garland's recordings is one of life's guilty pleasures for hordes of

jazz fans. By now, the Texan's cult following has probably adopted a secret hand-

shake. Garland's cheeky blues sense and hard-swinging style account in large part

for his popularity; the same elements that curried favor for his contemporary,

Horace Silver. Each artist is easily distinguishable from the other, however, for all

of their common bonds—Garland is pianistic even at his sassiest; Silver is raucous,

fighting a fixed-pitch instrument for the illusion of bent notes.

Garland's influences were tempered by the elegant touch of Nat "King" Cole. To his credit, Garland never indulged in relentless streams of eighth notes—the Bud Powell "lite" style—that so many pianists of his generation played. The ubiquitous Powell is there, however, but subtly disguised by lines punctuated with triplets, sixteenths, and a judicious use of space. Other *sui generis* ingredients include block chord voicings (a melody above middle C stated in octaves divided by fifths and supported by triad harmony in the tenor register) and a built-in, left-hand accompaniment cheerfully chording on the upbeats of two and four.

Dallas-born Garland flirted with the clarinet and the alto saxophone in his teens. His more serious aspirations as a professional boxer at the time were sidetracked by the draft. While serving in the Army, he took up the piano at the non-prodigy age of twenty. Notwithstanding the late start, he was to become a fluent technician. Discharged in '44, he was already holding his own as pianist in a group led by "Hot Lips" Page. In '46, he joined the Billy Eckstine big band, which featured several key members of the emerging bebop school—an experience that had a lasting impact on his style.

Gigs with Coleman Hawkins, Roy Eldridge, and other icons followed, but it was his long stint with Miles Davis's quintet (1955–59) that brought him fame— Garland, together with bassist Paul Chambers and drummer Philly Joe Jones, were known as the rhythm section of the period. Their spectacular synergy as a unit, with or without Davis, can be heard on many Prestige recordings. West Coast altoist, Art Pepper, borrowed them for his *Art Pepper Meets the Rhythm Section* (Contemporary). The session's pianist turned in some of his best work to date as accompanist and soloist.

After leaving Davis, Garland recorded extensively, sometimes with horns (*Red Alert*, Galaxy Records, 1977, with Harold Land, Nat Adderley, and Ira Sullivan, who is a stand-out), but mostly with trios.

He returned to his native Dallas upon the death of his mother in '65, subsequently remaining there through the end of his life. Except for occasional recording dates in New York, he retired from the scene, disappointing a fanbase that included several notable jazz pianists. It is said that he did not own a piano at the time of his death.

Photo: Lee Tanner/Jazz Image

11 McCoy Tyner

(1938 -   )

During his formative years in his native Philadelphia, McCoy Tyner was privileged

to have no less than Bud and Richie Powell as neighbors. They occasionally

dropped in during the rehearsals of a seven-piece band, led by the fledgling

pianist, to shine a light on some of the dark corners of the creative process. Tyner

was also learning his craft with a private teacher and attending the West

Philadelphia Music School. Later study at the Granoff Music School provided a

solid grounding in harmony and theory.

Word of the promising youngster reached fellow Philadelphian Benny Golson, who hired Tyner for his newly formed jazztet. Tyner made his first recordings with Golson, including the crossover hit "Killer Joe." Within a short time, John Coltrane, another product of the City of Brotherly Love, recruited Tyner for a quartet that included Elvin Jones and Jimmy Garrison. Coltrane and Tyner shared the common bond of refusing to be standard-issue beboppers. It was this unit under Coltrane's inspired and inspiring leadership that let the genie out of the bottle for Tyner. When he left the epochal group, Tyner's style was a boiling cauldron of quartal harmony (chords built on intervals of the fourth), dense textures, and effusive modal scales.

However, his career as a leader floundered in the late '60s and early '70s—at one point, he considered driving a hack to support his family. These were the days of under-promotion in jazz, but it didn't help that Tyner was as disinterested (read: hostile) in electronic trends as he is today.

Aggressive promotion for a series of recordings for Milestone (among them, *Song for My Lady*, *Song for the New World*, and the two-disc sets *Enlightenment '73* and *Atlantis*) rekindled his career and firmly established Tyner as the most influential pianist since Bill Evans.

Tyner's increasingly percussive approach to the piano and imaginative composing and arranging skills can be found on recordings with larger ensembles as diverse as a string section and a wordless chorus. *What the World Needs Now: The Music of Burt Bacharach*, with symphony orchestra arranged by John Clayton, makes for easy listening of a higher order.

Tyner's many solo piano recordings are intensely personal. An honest, exuberant virtuoso emerges, compensating for the sometimes poker-faced solemnity that mars some of his group work.

A very spiritual man, Tyner converted to the Islamic faith as a teenager when he took the name Sulaimon Saud.

Photo: Redferns Music Picture Library

12 Gene Harris

(1933 - 2000)

Long before the rubric "world music" made it possible for musicians with little or no affinity for the blues to sustain successful careers in what was once unequivocally called jazz, Gene Harris was a blues-based, groove-oriented player, and proud of it. For Harris, Indian ragas, Celtic folk songs, and other pan-cultural elements were all very well in themselves, but anathema to jazz tradition. Like the early bluesmen who played on battered pianos in mining camps and juke joints, Harris mimicked train whistles, suggested the bent notes of guitarists, and reflected his deep roots in the black sanctified church. His infectious, direct-address style made Harris a popular recording artist, but he remains underrated by the critics.

A native of Benton Harbor, Michigan, the self-taught Harris started playing at the age of four. Exposure to the family's boogie-woogie records by Albert Ammons and Pete Johnson led to important trial-and-error emulation. He played for local church services as a seven-year-old, and at twelve, he had his own radio show.

In 1951, Harris joined the Army where he learned to read music as a member of the 82nd Airborne Band. After his discharge in 1953, he toured with various groups, then formed the Four Sounds, a piano trio with tenor saxophone. When a suitable hornman couldn't be found, the group was renamed the Three Sounds. Their recording debut on Blue Note (1958) was a great success, and deservedly so. Out of print now for many years, it is a glaring omission in Blue Note's other-wise well-chosen series of classic reissues.

The Three Sounds were a blue-chip name in jazz circles for the next twenty years, even with varying personnel changes. Harris kept the unit's blues, bop, and gospel policy intact except for a few jazz/rock recordings in the mid '70s. Retired from touring from 1977 through 1980, he was content with his duties as musical direc-tor for the Idanha Hotel in Boise, Idaho, until a contract with Concord Records rekindled his career. Harris's recordings on the mainstream-friendly label are among his best. *Live at Town Hall in NYC* and *World Tour 1990* feature him in big-band settings with stellar soloists. A solo recital on *Maybeck* (1992), shows Harris none the worse for wear in the absence of a rhythm section, and *Alley Cats* (1998), recorded near the end of a bravely fought battle with a lingering illness that Harris eventually lost, is a romping gem.

Harris's idols were clear—Oscar Peterson and Erroll Garner. Harris fell short of Peterson's masterful technique, but matched him in the ability to generate enough momentum to sail a clipper ship. Garner's slaphappy influence runs deep as a philosophical role model, rather than a style for replication. Typically, Harris's closing comment each evening was, "If you leave here with a smile on your face, remember that Gene Harris put it there."

Photo: Redferns Music Picture Library

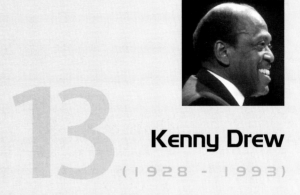

13 Kenny Drew

(1928 - 1993)

Kenny Drew spent half of his life abroad. Once a fixture on the high end of New York's hard bop scene, he moved his base of operations first to Paris (1961), and then permanently to Copenhagen (1964). Like many of the African-American jazzmen before and after him, Drew's solution to the problem of his homeland's indigenous racism was expatriation. The loss to American jazz is clear on even a cursory hearing of his trio records for Riverside in the '50s. Also relinquished to more welcoming cultures was the deft accompanying skill Drew brought to the table on John Coltrane's *Blue Train* (Blue Note, 1957).

Born in New York City, Drew started private piano instruction at the age of five. His mother, a classical pianist, provided additional coaching. At twelve, he was imitating the styles of Fats Waller and Art Tatum. After graduating from New York's Music and Art High School as the de facto boogie-woogie king of the student body, he joined the burgeoning bebop movement.

With his best Bud Powell impression in tow, Drew took his first professional job—an engagement as an accompanist for Pearl Primus, a dancer on 52nd Street. Between sets, under the myriad blinking neon signs on "the street," he formed a friendship with Al Haig. Haig occasionally let Drew sit in on the bandstand with Charlie Parker. The two pianists' association may have suggested Drew's escape from the overwhelming influence of Powell. Haig's playing was a refreshing alternative to the founding father's of bebop piano, while still remaining faithful to the essentials of the new language. Drew's later use of wide intervals and perky rhythmic ideas for melodic fodder are as likely to have begun with Haig as with anyone.

In 1950, trumpeter Howard McGhee hired Drew, initiating an iconic list of leaders in the pianist's early résumé, which includes Coleman Hawkins, Lester Young, Charlie Parker, Art Blakey, and Buddy DeFranco. By the mid '50s, Drew was recording often and well, leading his own trios. As a soloist, he approached theme statements with subtle harmonizations, while adhering to the composer's original melody with an almost canine loyalty. These qualities set *Pal Joey* (Original Jazz Classics, 1957) apart from the many Broadway-goes-jazz recordings of the late '50s. (André Previn's arrangements for his own *Pal Joey* album from the same year seem a bit overloaded and self-consciously "arty" in the light of Drew's interpretations—epic-scale plays performed on a rather small stage.)

Drew was not entirely bereft of the company of American jazzmen after his defection to Paris. Powell, whose influence on Drew remained substantial, was living there. Others, like Johnny Griffin, Kenny Dorham, Dexter Gordon, and Ben Webster, were either residents or touring soloists. Drew joined the house rhythm section in Copenhagen's Jazzhus Montmartre, where he continued to interface with old associates from his New York days. In 1989, he recorded *Recollections* (Timeless), one of the best outings of his last years. Drew is survived by a talented pianist son, Kenny Drew, Jr.

Photo: Lee Tanner/Jazz Image

14 Hampton Hawes
(1928 - 1977)

A product of the City of Angels, Hampton Hawes's best playing poses an irrefutable argument against pigeonholing West Coast jazzmen as cooler, more restrained types than their East Coast counterparts. One searches far and wide to find harder-swinging, fire-in-the-belly piano playing than Hawes's at full tilt.

Hawes began a lifelong commitment to self-instruction at the age of nine, copying boogie-woogie patterns from recordings by Earl Hines and Albert Ammons. He heard a Charlie Parker record while attending junior high school (courtesy of classmate Eric Dolphy), and the bebop die was cast. A quick study, he was working with Big Jay McNeely while still in his mid-teens. Before his two-year hitch in the army (1952–54), he had passed through the bands of Dexter Gordon, Wardell Gray, and Shorty Rogers as a promising diamond-in-the-rough with an obvious Bud Powell influence. Hawes often said his Army years provided the pianos and enough isolation from the hurly-burly music scene to polish his playing and help him muster a personal imprint.

By '55, his recordings for Contemporary Records (*The Trio, Vols. 1–3*, re-issued on OJC), created a sensation in the jazz world. Critic Nat Hentoff, in a review for *Downbeat* magazine, was moved to write: "He [Hawes] comes through here as potentially the most vital young pianist since Bud Powell in terms of fire, soul, beat and guts." At his peak, before his career was interrupted by a ten-year prison sentence for possession of heroin (and for which he was pardoned by President Kennedy in '64), Hawes had managed to reduce Powell's influence to an echo while still retaining his mentor's intensity and unbuttoned energy.

The bluesy, mature Hawes style is easily identified. His left hand stabs at acrid intervals like most bop pianists, but with more selectivity in the voice leading. His long-limbed, staccato phrases are punctuated by exploiting time durations and range shifts, much in the way a good speaker avoids making a flat Rotarian speech: a short pause above the general range serves as a comma—a long pause below the line, a period. He also serves up strategically placed couplings in each hand of a primary chord tone with its upper fifth and… voila, we have an exclamation point.

Horace Silver was somewhat affected by Hawes's earthy sermonettes, but worked within the comfort zone of his own material. Solo space was shared with the other members of his quintet. Hawes, the more pronounced virtuoso of the two, played standards almost exclusively and exposed himself to constant, demanding scrutiny as the primary soloist in a trio.

Hawes's post-pardon recordings show a marked decline in style and content. He flirted with electronic instruments and sometimes crossed over into the pop market. *Raise Up Off Me*, an embittered autobiography, was released shortly before he died of a stroke.

Photo: Lee Tanner/Jazz Image

15 Thelonious Monk

(1917 - 1982)

Long before San Juan Hill on New York City's Upper West Side became the site of

Lincoln Center, Thelonious Monk was growing up there among such neighbors as

James P. Johnson and Willie "The Lion" Smith. Not originally a New Yorker (he was

born in Rocky Mount, North Carolina), Monk's access to those stride piano leg-

ends is manifest at times in his piano style.

The future high priest of bebop started out as a rent-party piano player and accompanist for his mother's singing in church. By the early '40s, he was the house pianist at Minton's Playhouse in Harlem. There he, Charlie Parker, and Dizzy Gillespie rode the same horse toward a revolution in music.

Monk's inimitable traits are evident on his earliest recordings—an unorthodox piano technique laced with the stride style of his early mentors, the free use of dissonance, and an angular harmonic sense. His improvisations are sometimes comparable to the willy-nilly flight path of a deflated balloon.

Splayed hands probing the posteriors of chords with little concern for feats of derring-do are unlikely candidates for emulation. Traces of Monk's approach to the piano are scant (Randy Weston, Dollar Brand, Cecil Taylor, and a few others). None of his progeny have made the cut for this book. Comparisons with Ellington both as pianist and composer are not without merit, but Ellington's piano playing was notier, more romantic, more melodically conservative than Monk's. Ellington often explored extended forms as a composer. Monk was never distracted from simple ternery forms.

Such a style did not readily connect with a very large audience. Indeed, success and acclaim eluded Monk until his recordings for Riverside in the late '50s. Epithets like "eccentric genius" and "a true original" began to appear in his record reviews. Crowds flocked to hear him at the Five Spot in Greenwich Village, where he sustained long and frequent engagements. His popularity peaked on Columbia recordings in the '60s. Thereafter, his scattered history on smaller labels reflects the public's waning interest in his work.

Monk is one of jazz's greatest composers. Sooner or later every jazz musician must come to terms with "'Round Midnight," "Epistophy," "Misterioso," "Ruby, My Dear," etc.

Perhaps these days of fashionably eccentric celebrities will eventually minimize the lunatic image that has done such a disservice to Monk's legacy. A long Vandyke beard, bamboo-frame sunglasses, and a hat suggesting a papal miter, can now be dismissed as a mainstream appearance for an artist. True enough, Monk himself added more than a few bats-in-the-belfry when he found it commercially expedient; i.e., spinning himself like a top on and off stage, and posing for a record cover (*Underground*, Columbia) seated at a piano, a machine gun slung over his shoulder, surrounded by enough munitions to fill an armory.

The jazz community has hosted, and financially rewarded, its share of showmen (Armstrong, Gillespie, Waller) without the patronizing blowback on their work that had once been Monk's fate. Monk's playing is much more than a reflection of an arcane persona; it is vital, swinging jazz.

Photo: Alan Nahigian

16 Ahmad Jamal

(1930 -   )

The commercial hit album, *Ahmad Jamal at the Pershing* (Chess, 1958), was no fluke.

Four more Jamal albums appeared high on *Billboard*'s national pop album charts

well into the late '60s. His astonishing outreach—considering the laconic, under-

stated style he sported at the time—included non-musicians and musicians alike.

Jamalisms can be heard in the playing of Cedar Walton, Red Garland, and Wynton

Kelly. His vampy, two-beat grooves, four-bar tags, and repertoire staples were

recruited by no less than Miles Davis. Davis recorded Jamal's composition "New

Rhumba" in a Gil Evans arrangement as early as 1957.

Jamal adopted a Muslim name in early adulthood after converting to the Islamic faith. He was born Fritz Jones in Pittsburgh, a city that has produced a horde of remarkable jazz piano players. (Jazz historians, please note: there is a Pittsburgh school of jazz pianists, and its enrollment is appreciably larger in number than the much touted Detroit school of Hank Jones, Tommy Flanagan, Roland Hanna, etc.) Classically trained from the age of seven by, among others, Mary Caldwell Dawson, the founder of the first black opera company in America, Jamal was playing Liszt études at eleven. His first important exposure as a professional was in Chicago as a member of the Four Strings. Losing a member (violinist Joe Kennedy), it became the Three Strings, and ultimately, the Ahmad Jamal Trio. Most of Jamal's chart-busting recordings were made with Israel Crosby on bass and Vernel Fournier on drums—one of his best trios. Their symbiosis, so essential to the leader's tight, interdependent arrangements, suggested a unit twice its size. Considering the profligacy of Jamal's later albums with fairly disengaged rhythm sections, it can be said that he was once over-recorded.

Jamal's piano style is very personal, but the early influence of Erroll Garner (a Pittsburgh high school chum), still lingers. Garner's witty phrasing is recalled without the doggie-sweater cuteness of lesser Garnerians. His lower-register recitatives, swinging, orchestral approach, and contrasting dynamics are all redolent of the composer of "Misty." but Jamal is his own man in matters of melody and harmony. In theme statements, his single-note lines anticipate phrases two and sometimes four bars ahead of time, allowing the errant snippets to tweak the harmony of the moment in interesting ways. The process blurs the division between the head and the improvised segment. Other harmonic adventures frequently utilize the pedal point, a device wherein a sustained or repeated bass note grounds the free exploration of super-imposed chords.

His playing since the mid '70s is richer and fuller than before (*I Remember Duke, Hoagy and Strayhorn*, Telarc, 1994). Jamal now bristles at the mention of the word "jazz," preferring the term "contemporary American music." Still a favorite with listeners of every stripe, his dignified persona can be seen performing at festivals, concert halls, and nightclubs throughout the world.

Photo: Frank Driggs Collection

17 Billy Taylor

(1921 -   )

Few jazz players can match Billy Taylor's record of service to the music—not only as a high-tier performing artist, but also as a valued educator and articulate spokesman. Originally from North Carolina, Taylor grew up in Washington, D.C. His interest in the piano was marginal until he heard Fats Waller and Art Tatum on recordings. Later, duly armed with private studies (including instruction with Henry Grant—Duke Ellington's only formal teacher), and a bachelor of music degree from Virginia State College, he set his sights for New York.

He worked with Ben Webster at the Three Deuces on 52nd Street (1944). Other heavy-hitters appear on his early résumé—Stuff Smith, Billie Holiday, and Dizzy Gillespie. An inveterate student, he took the advice of Teddy Wilson and studied with Richard McClanahan. Taylor worked briefly in Machito's band (1946) before returning to the Three Deuces with Slam Stewart. After a European tour with Don Redman, he freelanced in Paris.

Stateside again in 1950, he led a quartet which became, under Artie Shaw's leadership, the third and last incarnation of Shaw's Gramercy Five. Taylor left the group to work as house pianist at Birdland (1951). In '52, he began fronting trios, an ensemble type he prefers to this day for recordings and live appearances.

Taylor's style is a highly polished conception of bebop filtered through the prism of Bud Powell. The bebop torch burns brightly, even on his most recent recordings (*Music Keeps Us Young*; *Ten Fingers, One Voice*; Arcadia, 1996). Neither an innovator nor strikingly original, Taylor has other compensating strengths: a solid sense of continuity, a commitment to swing for the fences, and a true jazz ear for harmony, regardless of borrowings from Ravel and other impressionists. For all of Taylor's knowledge of European classical tradition (he ultimately earned a PhD in music from the University of Massachusetts in '75), his work is never self-consciously Euro-centric.

Taylor is convinced that jazz can be taught. He maintains that there is an overly reverential tendency among teachers to harbor the music's innards as though they were the secrets of a lost civilization. To prove the point, he wrote excellent pedagogical articles for *Downbeat*, *Esquire*, and *The Saturday Review of Literature*. He also co-founded Jazzmobile (1965), which gives free concerts in the street. *Jazz Piano* (1982), his fine instructional book, is based on the thirteen-segment NPR series "Taylor Made Piano."

Very telegenic, with an appealing employee-of-the-month smile, Taylor was the musical director for David Frost's TV show (1969–72), and arts correspondent for Charles Kuralt's "Sunday Morning" on CBS (1981).

The veteran pianist has completely recovered from a recent stroke, but is disinclined to rest on his laurels. As the current artistic advisor for Kennedy Center Jazz in Washington, D.C., he shows no signs of retirement.

Photo: Lee Tanner/Jazz Image

18 Horace Silver

(1928 -)

For all practical purposes, Horace Silver is a self-taught pianist. Except for random lessons with a few local teachers in his native Norwalk, Connecticut, the primary schooling of the future "Hard Bop Grandpop" came from the recordings of Charlie Parker, Bud Powell, and Thelonious Monk, dissected at half speed, and the purchase of a basic harmony book. During his high school years, the playing of Lester Young also led to self-instruction on the tenor saxophone.

The pianist's debut recordings in 1951 were made in the employ of the ultimate Lester Young disciple, Stan Getz. Silver's composition, "Split Kick," is a highlight of the proceedings. An attractive "head," its Latin elements foreshadow many of his later brainchildren: "Señor Blues," "Nica's Dream," and "Song for My Father."

After leaving Getz, Silver jealously guarded the original voice he heard emerging on his trio sessions for Blue Note (1952–53), and closeted his record player to avoid the influence of other pianists. His unique musical persona was fully developed before he left the various incarnations of drummer Art Blakey's Jazz Messengers in '56.

Silver's bluesy, mature style was as naughty as a women's prison flick. No longer a Bud Powell knock-off, other qualities came to light. He hot-wired snarky, right-hand lines with a kind of bebop reconfiguration of the thumb tone—an old Broadway rehearsal pianist's device for suggesting a fuller accompaniment by the insertion of a tenor-register inner voice with the thumb of the right hand. Silver transferred a similar procedure to his left hand. A quirky simplicity vaguely echoes Monk, but owes as much to speech-inflected horn phrasing. The style, overall, does not pander to devotees of super-chops.

With no small input from Blakey, Silver wrote the constitution for a driving gospel and blues antidote to the more ethereal cool school of the mid '50s, which came to be known as hard bop or soul jazz. He fully enforced its ideologies in his own quintets through the years. Future luminaries Freddie Hubbard, Woody Shaw, Randy Brecker, Junior Cook, Wayne Shorter, and Joe Henderson apprenticed in the group's trumpet and tenor sax frontline. The leader featured many of his contributions as a composer to the standard jazz repertoire: "Doodlin'," "Opus de Funk," and "Filthy McNasty" among them.

Something of Silver's essence was lost in the translation to the larger ensembles of his '70s Blue Note sessions as he attempted to broaden his palette. *Silver 'n' Brass*, *Silver 'n' Voices*, and *Silver 'n' Strings Play the Music of the Spheres* received little more than a tepid response from his most devoted fans. By the last decade of the century, a growing interest in quasi-religious metaphysics led to the lamentable recording project *Rockin' with Rachmaninoff* (Bop City)—a fantasy wherein a celestial Duke Ellington introduces his equally celestial Russian colleague to several jazz legends residing in heaven.

Silver still manages to redeem himself on occasion with piano solos that turn up the heat, even in the most doubtful settings.

Photo: Alan Nahigian

19 Hank Jones

(1918 -)

New York's 52nd Street offered a plethora of talented bebop pianists in the mid

'40s. Inevitably, a kind of cross-fertilization took place among the young lions as

each struggled to find his own identity within the standard-bearing parameters

set by Bud Powell.

Working on "the street" after apprenticeships in his hometown of Pontiac, Michigan and nearby Detroit, Jones's solution to the Powell problem was suggested by the exposure to Al Haig's playing in the tightly clustered clubs along the famed strip. Like Haig, Jones worked out a timeless style by fusing the older traditions of Art Tatum and Teddy Wilson with a generous sampling of the newer ideas. Jones still shares common bonds with Haig; a velvet touch, a preference for fuller left-hand voicings than other pianists, and a standards-centric repertoire. He is, however, a superior harmonist and the stronger swinger by far. Jones added other components to the mix: a bluesy elegance (the ability to bump and grind "on pointe," as it were) and a sly sense of humor.

The former Midwesterner appeared with 52nd Street's top attractions from 1944–48. He began recording for Norman Granz in the late '40s, and toured with the impresario's Jazz at the Philharmonic until '53. Taking part in the nightly cutting contests that Granz staged between Roy Eldridge, Lester Young, Charlie Shavers, Dizzy Gillespie, and Charlie Parker sharpened Jones's already burgeoning versatility. Ella Fitzgerald, a Philharmonic staple in those days, was the first of many vocalists to utilize Jones's sensitivity as an accompanist. He has since rendered tasteful backup for Billy Eckstine, Sarah Vaughan, Chris Connor, and, more recently, Abbey Lincoln (*When There Is Love*, Verve, 1994).

A busy freelancer throughout the '50s and '60s, Jones's busy schedule included two recording sessions with his younger brothers, trumpeter Thad and drummer Elvin (*Keepin' Up with the Joneses*, 1958, reissued on Verve, 1999; and *Elvin!* on Riverside). The pianist's non-generic intros jumpstart several of the tracks. Thad wrote similar intros, fastidiously harmonizing cycles of fifths against upward-spiraling chromatic lines, for his well-known big band charts. The true progenitor must remain a mystery.

Jones's sixteen years as a CBS staff musician (1959–75), his long run as pianist/conductor in the Fats Waller musical *Ain't Misbehavin'*, and his recordings with bassist Ron Carter and drummer Tony Williams in the Great Jazz Trio verify his enormous contextual range. He can also be heard, to protean advantage, in recorded piano duets with Tommy Flanagan, John Lewis, George Shearing, and Marion McPartland.

Still active at the time of this writing (he celebrated his 85th birthday in the summer of '03 at the Blue Note, surrounded by a veritable who's who of the jazz community), Jones begins the genealogy of the Detroit piano school, which continues with Tommy Flanagan, Barry Harris, and Sir Roland Hanna.

Photo: Lee Tanner/Jazz Image

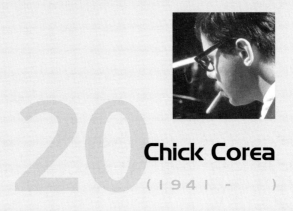

20 Chick Corea

(1 9 4 1 -   )

Chick Corea was born in Chelsea, Massachusetts. He began playing at the age of

four, studying with his father, a professional trumpet player and bandleader. A few

years later, the tutoring chores were passed on to a classical teacher in the Boston

area. Corea immersed himself in the piano literature of Bach, Beethoven, and

Chopin while lending an ear to his father's jazz record collection, which included

Bud Powell's first recordings for Blue Note. By his mid-teens, when his classical stud-

ies had ended, he was transcribing Horace Silver solos and leading a small group for

dances. The group's "Silver" streak was reserved for appearances at local jazz clubs.

After graduating high school, Corea moved to New York City where he attended Columbia University and the Julliard School of Music. He left Julliard in the early '60s, when the demanding curriculum of a piano major intruded on his gigs in the Latin bands of Mongo Santamaria and Willie Bobo. Corea freelanced with Blue Mitchell, Herbie Mann, Stan Getz, and Sarah Vaughan until he joined Miles Davis in 1968. Davis was influential in converting him to electronic keyboards. Corea's performances on the Fender Rhodes electric piano add considerable interest to some of the best recordings from Davis's fusion period (*In a Silent Way*, *Bitches Brew*, Columbia Records).

Leaving Davis in 1970, Corea formed the acoustic trio Circle, which later became a quartet with the addition of saxophonist Anthony Braxton. Avant-garde audiences cheered its extended freeform improvisations. Corea soon resigned from Circle, however, finding the context too exclusionary and elitist. His next band, Return to Forever (1972), reflected his growing interest in Scientology, a philosophical belief system based on the value of communication. The band's Latin and jazz/rock orientation snagged a huge following, and the leader was playing electric keyboards again. Corea's compositions from this period ("Spain," "500 Miles High," "La Fiesta"), and others that followed, earned their creator a privileged status as one of the most popular jazz composers of the post-bop generation.

Since disbanding RTF in 1980, Corea has led the Elektric Band, the Akoustic Band, and more recently, Origin. The shifting personnel and instrumentation, whether acoustic, electronic or both, are designed to appease the leader's restless creativity. In 1992, Corea founded Stretch Records, a bully pulpit for himself (*Time Warps*, 1995) and other artists such as Eddie Gomez, John Patitucci, and Robben Ford.

Corea, Herbie Hancock, and Keith Jarrett were the predominant movers and shakers of jazz piano in the '70s and '80s. The common bonds between them are tenuous beyond their shared histories as classically trained virtuosos and ex-Miles Davis sidemen. Each has made a vital contribution in his own way—Corea by the lavish use of Bartókian ornamentation (his whole-step grace notes are an interesting Transylvanian alternative to the more familiar half-step model) and a time sense based on the duple and triple meters of Latin music; Hancock by adding a polytonal dimension to the language of bebop; Jarrett by the coupling of asymmetrical phrases with other bar-line blurring devices to surprise the unwary listener.

Photo: Jose M. Horna

21 Tete Montoliu

(1933 - 1997)

Of the trinity of blind pianists represented in this collection (Montoliu, George Shearing, and Lennie Tristano), Tete Montoliu is the only one to endure a further disadvantage—growing up under the repressive regime of Generalissimo Francisco Franco. Born in Barcelona, Spain, the son of an oboist/English horn player in the city's symphony orchestra, Montoliu learned to read music in Braille at the age of seven. He set his cap for a jazz career inspired by Duke Ellington records and some jamming with the great tenor saxophonist Don Byas, who lived briefly in the Montoliu household in 1943. By the late '40s, he had completed his studies at the Barcelona Conservatory, and was already feeling the pinch of the Franco government's hostility to any form of free, creative expression. His early career is marked by the struggle for a livelihood in Spain's meager jazz community.

Conditions began to relax and Montoliu recorded with Lionel Hampton in Madrid in 1956. In '58, he appeared at the Cannes Festival with Doug Watkins and Art Taylor. His growing reputation as a strong soloist and vacuum cleaner-eared accompanist put him on the A-list for recording calls with visiting American soloists throughout Europe and Scandinavia. Montoliu took leave periodically from Satchmo, a small Barcelona nightclub, to meet the demands of his busy schedule.

Trio sessions began to appear under Montoliu's name. Among them, *A Tot Jazz* (recorded in 1965 and reissued as two CDs on Fresh Sound, 1993) is typical of his playing in the '60s—standards filtered through a witty, high-grade bebop sensibility. In the '70s, he often recorded in Denmark with Niels-Henning Ørsted Pedersen, a bassist who likes nothing more than playing with pianists blessed with stupendous technique. Their *Tete a Tete* (Steeplechase, 1976) is a particularly fruitful collaboration.

Montoliu selectively adopted the new developments in jazz piano as the years went on. He took from Bill Evans, McCoy Tyner, and Herbie Hancock only the ideas that didn't imperil his bebop roots. The stylistic updating allowed him to play with avant-garde-ists like Archie Shepp and Anthony Braxton. During his second of two visits to the U.S. (1967 and 1979), he recorded *Lunch in L.A.* (Contemporary), which includes a very au courant piano duet with Chick Corea.

The track reveals an interesting role reversal: Montoliu is the more blues-based of the two; Corea the more "Spanish."

For all of Montoliu's profound ties with American music, he chose to remain in Europe. A proud Catalan (Catalans consider themselves an ethnic breed apart from other Spaniards), he was never tempted to leave his beloved Barcelona for any sustained period of time. A verbal exchange between Montoliu and Ben Webster overheard at a recording session illustrates the pianist's fierce nationalism and touches on his musical affinities: Webster: " This Spanish fella swings like no other pianist in Europe." Montoliu: " I'm no Spaniard, I'm a Catalan. Don't you know? All Catalans are colored."

Montoliu's brisk career pace never slackened until the mid '90s, when he was diagnosed with lung cancer and experiencing severe hearing loss. He died shortly after a piano duo engagement he was unable to fulfill at the San Sebastian Jazz Festival. His duo partner would have been Hank Jones.

Photo: Frank Driggs Collection

22 Phineas Newborn, Jr.

(1931 - 1989)

Phineas Newborn, Jr. was never forgiven for his super-chops. In jazz, the ability to

overcome the piano's most challenging pitfalls tends to disqualify the player from

any association with emotional commitment or "soul." Newborn's career was all

but sabotaged by such all sizzle/no steak allegations. Even the endorsements of

Oscar Peterson (no stranger to the same charges), Count Basie, and jazz critics

Ralph Gleason and Nat Hentoff did little to mitigate Newborn's virtuoso albatross.

Born in Whiteville, Tennessee but Memphis-bred, Newborn could play a number of brass and reed instruments before he finished high school—an ability he shared with Lennie Tristano. As a teenager, he devoured classical piano literature, adopting the Lisztian practice of executing intricate melodic lines at the double and occasionally triple octave, which was to become a highlight of Newborn's mature style. Recordings by Art Tatum and Bud Powell were deconstructed, not for purposes of slavish imitation, but to serve as frames of reference.

Before his much ballyhooed appearance leading a trio at Manhattan's Basin Street East, his résumé as a sideman included stints with Lionel Hampton (1950 and 1952) and rhythm and blues bands led by Willis Jackson and B.B. King. The Basin Street engagement led to recordings on Atlantic and RCA, which are not to be believed for driving swing, harmonic imagination, and, yes, commanding technique. *While My Lady Sleeps* (RCA, now reissued on Collectables Jazz Classics), a ballad session with strings arranged by Denis Farnon, showcases a pianist dissatisfied with mere greeting-card sentimentality. His hair-trigger time and innate blues sense result in contemplative and poetic performances without a hint of mawkishness.

Two other recordings from his New York days are notable: *We Three* (Prestige) in 1958, and a collaboration with bassist Charlie Mingus for the soundtrack of John Cassavettes's edgy film *Shadows* during the same year.

Newborn's work began a slow, steady decline after he moved to Los Angeles in '61. Emotional illness (for which he was admitted to Camarillo State Hospital), a hand injury, and critical ennui took their toll on a career that once seemed so promising. Both Newborn and Hampton Hawes's periodic disappearances (the latter's due to drug addiction) robbed the L.A. jazz scene of two of its best pianists.

The sessions of Newborn's last years are disappointing. A wearing sameness of insipid ballad and middle-ground tempos pervades them. He appears to have taken his negative press to heart, reducing his fleet-fingered lines to a minimum. In '87, two years before his death, he was rumored to be recording sonatas by the eccentric Russian composer Alexander Scriabin.

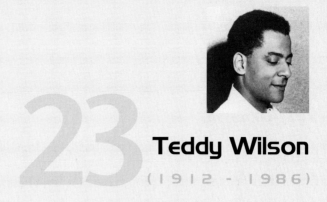

23 Teddy Wilson
(1912 - 1986)

The goalposts of jazz piano were moved forevermore when Teddy Wilson recorded in the mid '30s with the Benny Goodman Trio and Quartet. Wilson's consecutive "walking tenths," set against agile chromatic lines, broke ranks with the standard practices of his day and became a pervasive influence on other pianists. Not even his best disciples, however (Al Haig, Hank Jones, George Shearing), have replicated the grace and refinement of his playing.

Originally from Austin, Texas, Wilson grew up in Tuskegee, Alabama where he studied piano and violin at the Tuskegee Institute. He later enrolled in a general music curriculum at Talladega College. His professional career began in territorial bands led by Milt Senior and Speed Webb that toured the Midwest. During a stop in Toledo, Ohio in the early '30s, Wilson heard Art Tatum. Exposure to the Toledo-born icon's dazzling harmonic sense added a new and important dimension to Wilson's playing. A piano conception once rooted exclusively in Earl Hines's "trumpet style" morphed into a personal benchmark.

Wilson worked with the bands of Louis Armstrong, Jimmie Noone, and Benny Carter before making his first solo records in 1934. Judged unreleasable for being, ahem, "monotonous," their understated virtuosity did not escape the attention of influential Canadian journalist Helen Oakley. In spite of the racial obstacles of the '30s, Oakley convinced Benny Goodman that hiring Wilson, an African-American, for record dates and public appearances was somehow a marketable idea. The resulting Goodman/Wilson collaborations, begun in a trio with Gene Krupa and continued in a quartet (with the addition of Lionel Hampton), are now the stuff of jazz legend (*Benny Goodman: The Complete Small Group Sessions*, RCA, a three-CD set).

Goodman's high-profile units granted the pianist an enviable reputation as a soloist and accompanist. From 1935–42, Wilson led a cornucopia of record dates featuring vocals by Billie Holiday (among her best remembered), Helen Ward, and Lena Horne. Rife with top New York sidemen, the sessions are models of tasteful accompaniment and small-group swing. The leader's exceptional writing skills for the aforementioned went largely unnoticed; likewise, the scores for his short-lived big band of '39.

Wilson's popularity as a trio pianist survived the arrival of bebop and the Bud Powell generation. (Interestingly, Wilson was Powell's original influence.) He seldom revisited classics from his Goodman days on his later recordings; his repertoire was devoted mostly to standards by Gershwin, Porter, Arlen, et al (*Alone, Storyville*, 1983), and he mined endless riches from such songs. A fine teacher, numbering the gifted Dick Hyman among his pupils, Wilson has the unique distinction of being Julliard's first jazz piano teacher.

Photo: Frank Driggs Collection

24 Nat "King" Cole
(1917 - 1965)

Nat "King" Cole's defection from jazz in order to pursue the more lucrative career of a pop singer was not a clean break. The *rubato* phrasing of even his most saccharine vocal chartbusters could only have sprung from a jazz musician's maverick sense of time. Years after he had relinquished the piano, his fingers were still pickpocket-nimble when Stuff Smith, Sweets Edison, Willie Smith, Juan Tizol, and a marvelous rhythm section joined him for the eternally hip album *After Midnight*.

24

Alabama-born and Chicago-bred, Cole was a teenager when he left the Windy City to tour as the musical director with the revue Shuffle Along in 1936. The show folded in Los Angeles, but Cole liked the balmy climate enough to settle there. A welcome guest in local jam session clubs, he nonetheless endured long spates of unemployment until, in 1938, he decided to form a group with two of his most frequent jamming partners—guitarist Oscar Moore and bassist Wesley Prince. Cole exercised the privilege of his royal sobriquet, and he called it the King Cole Trio.

The Trio's success in the dance-oriented swing era proved that a bedrock-solid beat was not the exclusive domain of a big band. The unit's increasingly popular recordings, inspired other pianist/leaders (Art Tatum, Oscar Peterson, Page Cavanaugh, Lennie Tristano, André Previn) to copy its drummerless instrumentation.

Cole himself became a paradigm as a soloist. More velvet-handed than other descendents of Earl Hines, he tantalizingly dispensed his virtuosity in small doses. The centerpiece of his playing is a pulsing, riffy lyricism—think Oscar Peterson in his more restrained moments. Cole's unhurried use of space also resonated with Red Garland, Ahmad Jamal, and Tommy Flanagan; his sweet and sour chords with Bill Evans.

The trio began a long association with Capitol Records in '42 (eighteen CDs reissued on Mosaic). In '44, they took part in Norman Granz's early Jazz at the Philharmonic concerts. Although Cole was winning magazine jazz polls as a pianist (*Downbeat* and *Esquire*), his vocals—originally intended as a novelty—were catching on. "Straighten Up and Fly Right," his own composition and his first big hit as a songbird, sounded a death knell for the trio, which had undergone some personnel changes (Irving Ashby replacing Moore on guitar, Johnnie Miller and later Joe Comfort replacing Prince on bass), and was eventually dissolved in '51.

After Midnight (Capitol, 1956) is Cole's last hurrah as a jazz musician. Had he lived to a riper old age, he may have returned to his first love of jazz, given its more recent marketability. Before his death at age 45 from lung cancer, Cole was, and remains, one of the world's best-loved singers.

Photo: Frank Driggs Collection

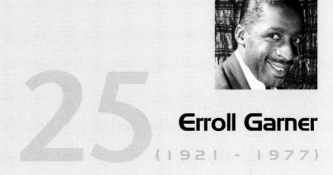

25 Erroll Garner

(1921 - 1977)

Much has been made of Erroll Garner's inability to read music. Since reading skill is not indispensable to jazz performance, the true measure of Garner's genius lies in how he reached such extraordinary creative heights with barely the capacity to identify basic scales and chord changes. Self-taught from the age of three, Garner's "training" was limited by choice to brief Q&A exchanges with his Pittsburgh school chums, Dodo Marmarosa and Billy Strayhorn. The scattershot musical data he received was apparently enough to ground a career for one of the best-loved pianists in jazz.

Garner left home, bound for New York in 1944. Gigs with Slam Stewart's trio at the Three Deuces on 52nd Street laid the foundation for a growing reputation. He began recording for small labels. His treatment of "Laura" (*Serenade to Laura*, Savoy), a new song when it debuted in the mid '40s, was a minor hit. In 1947, he cut four tracks for Dial Records with Charlie Parker (*Complete Charlie Parker on Dial*, a four-CD set reissued on Jazz Classics). Never really a bopper, Garner absorbed enough of the new language to stay current. By the early '50s, major labels were romancing him. *Concert by the Sea* (Columbia), a live recording, was a huge success. It has never been out of print since its release in 1956.

Under the astute management of Martha Glaser, Garner played to SRO audiences in prominent nightclubs and festivals. His fanbase embraced enough non-jazz listeners to justify frequent television appearances on the variety shows of Steve Allen, Ed Sullivan, and Perry Como. In '58, he was the first jazz artist to sign an exclusive contract with the celebrated classical music impresario Sol Hurok. As if further confirmation of his popularity was needed, he composed "Misty," one of the most recorded songs of all time.

Garner's piano style is full and rich. Jimmy Rowles called him "Ork," "because he sounded like an orchestra." His unique signature is clear in a few bars; whatever there once was of Earl Hines in his playing (note the Pittsburgh connection again), was gone by the late '40s. If Garner is anyone's heir-apparent, he is Fats Waller's, but only in that both artists are wholesalers of happy, unbuttoned joy. Even Garner's ballads are angstless celebrations of beauty. Their lush, impressionistic palette could soak a housepainter's drop cloth beyond redemption.

His intros are compressed overtures with atonal flirtings. Any heads-up for what is to follow is minimal but fascinating. Once in tempo, he thrums full chords in his left hand, four to the bar like a rhythm guitarist, while his right hand pairs astonishingly expressive lines and shaken, widespread chords. From intro to ending, the only predictable element in a Garner performance is that it will swing… really swing.

Garner's repertoire comprised a mammoth chunk of the *Great American Songbook*, including some of its more obscure entries. With the exception of a few departures from the original texts (he always repeated the first sixteen bars of "I'll Remember April"; and the surrogate bridge for "Will You Still Be Mine" bore no resemblance to Matt Dennis's smart-alecky creation), Garner showed absolute chapter-and-verse fidelity to the composers' intentions. For a non-reader with no recourse to consult published sheet music, his almost total musical recall is impressive. Never really a "finished" musician or virtuoso, Garner's many virtues should, nonetheless, be the envy of better-schooled pianists.

Photo: Frank Driggs Collection

102

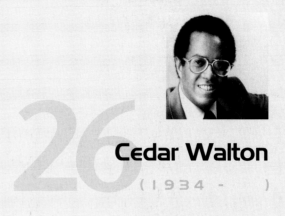

26 Cedar Walton

(1934 -)

Cedar Walton is one of the more interesting survivors of the hard bop piano turf wars. His style is personal, two-handed, and blues savvy. A bold but lucid harmonist, his chord substitutions are mercifully not guided by an ear, cocked to the wind, awaiting orders from the mother ship. His best work is informed by a thorough knowledge of the bellwethers of jazz piano tradition. Small wonder he is endorsed by Mary Lou Williams and Oscar Peterson.

Born in Dallas, Texas, Walton studied piano both with his mother and at the University of Denver Colorado. He was drafted in 1956, shortly after moving to New York City. Discharged in 1958, he joined trombonist J.J. Johnson's quartet (1958–60). (An interesting career footnote: although he was replaced for the final release by Tommy Flanagan, Walton was actually the first pianist to reckon with the slippery slope of John Coltrane's composition "Giant Steps" on the initial recording by the composer in 1959.)   After a year with the Art Farmer/Benny Golson Jazztet (1960–61), he assumed Bobby Timmons's old battle station in Art Blakey's hard-bopping Jazz Messengers. He left Blakey in '64 to freelance. As virtually the house pianist for Blue Note and Prestige Records through the remaining '60s, he recorded with a host of boldface names. He also made his first albums as a leader. Between sessions he accompanied vocalist Abbey Lincoln.

Walton was practically an expatriate in the '70s, working mostly in Europe. In 1975, he played a pivotal role in the formation of Eastern Rebellion, a piano trio augmented by tenor sax—the latter duties fulfilled at various times by Clifford Jordan, George Coleman, and Bob Berg. One of three co-op groups with which Walton has been associated, ER produced some memorable recordings (*First Set*, Steeplechase, 1977). Other ventures with the jazz/funk band Soundscapes and the neo-bop Timeless All-Stars were not always fruitful. Walton would lose his competitive edge in such decision-by-committee ensembles, and would generally take the path of least resistance. The experiences with diverse instrumentation, however, added new works to the catalogue of this gifted composer/arranger, which already boasted "Mosaic" (from his Blakey days), "Bolivia," and "Firm Roots."

In the '80s, Walton stepped up his trio recording schedule. There were some happy reunions as well with Abbey Lincoln and J.J. Johnson. The pianist had always spent quality time with Johnson, a musician who, like himself, reflected a composer's mind by his thoughtful, well-scaffolded approach to improvisation. In 1994, Walton was pianist/arranger for the Etta James album *Mystery Lady* (Private Stock), a Grammy Award-winning tribute to Billie Holiday.

Walton is not your garden variety, post-bop stylist; heard are traces of Herbie Hancock and McCoy Tyner, but he uses fourth interval voicings more sparingly, and his phrases neatly observe the bar lines. Mary Lou Williams approvingly referred to him in an interview as "the guy who plays like Bobby Timmons did"—Timmons being one of Walton's many channelings, determined by the context of the moment. (Walton was with Blakey's Messengers as the time.) When appropriate, he echoes all his instrument's predecessors by paraphrasings—not by literal mimicry. As a rule, his chord formations and somewhat angular lyricism bear his own imprint.

A first-rate solo pianist, Walton's Maybeck recital (Concord, 1992) is one of the high points of the series. He still records as a trio leader and appears in updated editions of Eastern Rebellion.

Photo: Frank Driggs Collection

27 Count Basie

(1904 - 1984)

Kansas City's teeming nightlife created a bull market for musicians from the late '20s through the 1930s. Count Basie, stranded there after the breakup of a theatrical troupe, was a long way from his native Red Bank, New Jersey. He easily found gainful employment in local theaters and bands. After a stint with Walter Page's Blue Devils (1928–29), he joined Benny Moten's band (1929–34). A standard-bearer for the riffy, loose-swinging traditions of Kansas City swing, Moten gradually hired Page and other key members of the Blue Devils, such as "Hot Lips" Page (no relation to Walter), Jimmy Rushing, and Lester Young.

When Moten died suddenly in 1935, Basie became the band's leader by the unanimous consent of its members—a decision based on his playing skill, authoritative baritone voice, and the personable manner he had groomed on the vaudeville circuit. In '36, record producer John Hammond heard the band on a radio broadcast. More than impressed, he convinced Basie to expand the band to twelve pieces and bring it to New York. The band's first success at the Roseland Ballroom was followed by a well-received engagement at the Famous Door nightclub. Basie's reputation was quickly secured.

The supreme irony of Basie's career as a bandleader is that a rag-tag "head" arrangement band, which was built around key soloists (Lester Young, Dickie Wells, "Sweets" Edison, etc.), evolved, through later emphasis on formal arrangements, into one of the finest precision ensembles in jazz history. Due praise for the Basie band is commonplace in jazz circles, but the leader's fine piano playing has almost consistently been overlooked.

Basie's brief solos are ingeniously terse and cherry-picked. His economy belies an alpha stride player who fortified the smattering of piano lessons of his youth with informal instruction by "tickler" icons Donald Lambert and Willie "The Lion" Smith. Fats Waller had also given him wise counsel in casual encounters at the organ of Harlem's Lincoln Theater.

It remained for jazz impresario Norman Granz to expose Basie's full glory as a soloist. He recorded the wary pianist without the encumbrance of his big band. The free-blowing formats of several *Basie Jam* albums, two duet sessions with Oscar Peterson, and a quartet gathering with Zoot Sims (all on Granz's Pablo label) reveal a chopsy, assertive Basie. His skill as a first-line comper is also more clearly audible in these sparer settings.

Keyboard comparisons with Duke Ellington are specious at best. Ellington's playing, although remarkably inventive, was secondary to his compositional interests and a unique distillation of his true instrument—the orchestra. Basie—no composer; self-deprecating to a fault—deferred to the band's many excellent scores and seldom featured himself.

Photo: Alan Nahigian

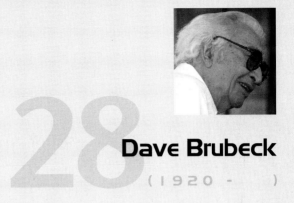

28 Dave Brubeck

(1920 -   )

Nothing arouses more suspicion in jazz circles than commercial success. An art form, ostensibly populist-proof, shrink-wrapped in the arcane and indecipherable, is bound to harbor a vigilante faction bent on discrediting artists who exceed a modest income—witness the demonization of Louis Armstrong, Miles Davis, Herbie Hancock, etc.

Dave Brubeck is one of the cash cows most consistently targeted by such a faction. Yet, the lanky Californian insists he won his considerable fanbase while remaining true to a basic jazz tenet—absolute improvisation. He has been less vocal about other essentials of the music (swinging—a sense of the blues). The problems with his detractors lie therein.

The son of a cattle rancher father who managed 45,000 acres of land in the Golden State and a concert pianist mother, Brubeck began playing in local bands at the age of thirteen. From 1938–42, he attended the College of the Pacific where, early on, he decided to switch his major from zoology to music. Postgraduate studies with Arnold Schoenberg and Darius Milhaud stimulated the young musician's predilection for bold, harmonic ideas.

In '46, freshly mustered out of the army, Brubeck formed an octet. His past encounters with Milhaud were reflected in arrangements that never met a polychord they didn't like. Audiences responded indifferently. After three lean years, the octet disbanded.

The next Brubeck-led incarnation, a trio, was mildly successful, but true celebrity and all of its perks came with the birth of a quartet in 1951 that featured altoist Paul Desmond. An alumnus of the octet, Desmond's playing was cerebral with a dusting of melancholy—Brubeck's mirror-image, in effect. Brubeck's face on a

Time magazine cover ('54) confirmed the quartet's popularity. Its wholesale offerings of dissonant counterpoint and polytonality enjoyed dramatic record sales (Fantasy and Columbia), and sold out houses in the group's live appearances. "Take 5," the hit Desmond opus in 5/4, was one of many experiments with odd time signatures. The leader's common-time compositions, "The Duke" and "In Your Own Sweet Way," were already jazz standards when he disbanded the group in '67 to concentrate on writing.

Brubeck's playing owes little to Tatum, Wilson, Powell, or any of the other mainstream stylists. Lennie Tristano is his closest equivalent; both pianists flirt with modern European classical techniques, and look upon improvisation as a challenge to create an impromptu whole greater than the sum of its parts. Brubeck, the lesser virtuoso of the two, explores a declamatory style built on sparsely noted riffs, rhythmic displacement, and dense chords; whereas, Tristano tends to frame his ideas around his humbling command of the instrument.

Since 1970, Brubeck has written several large-scale choral works. Now an octogenarian, he occasionally leaves the writing desk in his rural Connecticut home to tour with a quartet featuring his sons Darius, Chris, and Danny.

Photo: Alan Nahigian

29

Cyrus Chestnut
(1963 -   )

Cyrus Chestnut's playing has many strengths, not the least of which is its effective use of dynamics. He italicizes his ideas with masterfully controlled crescendos and decrescendos—a dramatic resource neglected by jazz pianists of most generations, but particularly his own. Like Ahmad Jamal (another purveyor of neatly terraced dynamics), Chestnut also knows the value of economy—the theory that less is more. The two pianists' common grounds in such matters are too deep-seated to be coincidental; Jamal, the elder of the pair by more than three decades, is clearly the matrix. Chestnut's sunny, uncomplicated style with its appealing gospel undercurrent makes a joyful noise in these secular times.

The grandson of a minister, Chestnut was born in Baltimore, Maryland. At the age of seven, he began studying the piano with his father. The religious services at Mt. Calvary Star Baptist Church provided an important early forum for his playing while he was still a boy. He later attended the Peabody Prep Institute and, while a student at the Berklee College of Music in Boston, he received three scholarships: the Eubie Blake (1982), the Oscar Peterson (1983), and the Quincy Jones (1984). In 1985, he graduated with a degree in jazz composition and arranging. After working with George Adams, he joined Jon Hendricks for appearances at several European festivals in 1989. He spent part of the same year with a quintet of young turks, under the co-leadership of Terence Blanchard and Donald Harrison.

Chestnut began to attract attention in the early '90s as Betty Carter's accompanist; but it was under the aegis of Wynton Marsalis—an influential leader with a revisionist mission to scrub clean all contemporary jazz with a mainstream jazz disinfectant—that he really came into his own. Since his stay as a member of Marsalis's Lincoln Center Jazz Orchestra (1995–96), he has led his own groups.

A very promising work-in-progress, Chestnut is still trying to find his reflection in the mirrors of legends. He has yet to tease out the unique voice suggested by his combined influences. To his credit, Chestnut's solos slyly crib from Bud Powell, Thelonious Monk, McCoy Tyner, and Ahmad Jamal without the blowback of incompatibility. His one constant, an honest gospel/blues component, seems to merge the disparate styles into a homogenous result. Indeed, it may be that Chestnut will come upon his own DNA—as Horace Silver, Bobby Timmons, and Gene Harris found theirs—under similar "soulful" auspices.

Recording for major labels has been a mixed blessing for Chestnut. The promotional advantages and prestige are not always counterweighted by the creative latitude a young artist needs to grow. *Blessed Quietness* (Warner Bros., 1996), is an engaging solo piano session nonetheless. The seasonal blight of an almost exclusive collection of Christmas carols can be an off-putting listening experience on a dog-day summer afternoon, but the playing is imaginatively self-contained and the dynamic range, as always with this artist, draws you in. He is Jamal's doppelganger again on *You Are My Sunshine* (Warner Bros., 2003). Some of Chestnut's chord voicings are frosted with a bit of irony… a harbinger of things to come?

A note for the cineaste/jazz fan: Chestnut, a big fellow with ample girth, cuts a Fats Waller-ish figure in Robert Altman's film, *Kansas City*.

Photo: Frank Driggs Collection

30 Lennie Tristano

(1919 - 1978)

An irony: one of jazz's true visionaries was sightless. Lennie Tristano was born in

Chicago during an influenza epidemic. The debilitating disease gradually affected

his eyesight, resulting in blindness at the age of eight. He began piano lessons at

seven. By the time he graduated from the American Conservatory of Music, he

was also proficient on several reed instruments, cello, guitar, and drums. A virtu-

oso pianist, Tristano morphed from an Earl Hines wannabe to a personal stylist

with an aversion to workaday values about harmony, time, and phrasing. In 1946,

after creating a stir in his hometown environs, he moved to New York, determined

to play a role in the gathering storm of bebop.

As the centerpiece of a Nat "King" Cole trio instrumentation (piano, bass, guitar), his complex, densely-voiced chords, and serpentine single-note lines attracted a small but dedicated coterie of mostly white musicians. Among the latter were saxophonists Warne Marsh and Lee Konitz, and guitarist Billy Bauer, who eventually became his students. With a growing reputation as a musical guru, the ex-Windy City pianist opened a studio in Queens in 1950—a surrender, no doubt, to his failure as a performer to woo the hoi polloi.

Tristano's efforts as a pianist and teacher were devoted to subverting traditional musical elements, which he felt contributed to dull, predictable improvisation: clear bar-line divisions, consistent time signatures, harmony dominated by the interval of the third, fixed tempos (in the ideal, at least), sustained from chorus to chorus. Perhaps to confirm his theories, his students were required to make a thorough study of the solos of Louis Armstrong, Lester Young, and Charlie Parker. The ultimate in conventional improvisation having thereby been well researched, the student might then be convinced that all efforts within those formulas were doomed to produce only shopworn clichés.

Tristano is under-recorded, but the meager pickings are uncommonly good. Of special interest are the seven historic records he made for Capitol in '49 (reissued on Definitive Records as *Lennie Tristano Supersonic*) with Marsh, Konitz, Bauer, and a sparkling rhythm section. On two of the tracks, "Intuition" and "Digression," the musicians were given no set key, melody, chord sequence, or tempo. This practice predates Ornette Coleman's similar experiments in the late '50s and the "free jazz" of the '60s. On another prophetic session in '55 (*Lennie Tristano*, Atlantic), he doctored the tapes by speeding up prerecorded rhythm tracks and dubbing his solos over them to blur what he felt was the tyranny of bar lines. Such technological shenanigans are now fashionable on recordings.

Other dubbings and tamperings occur on "Turkish Mambo" and the moving tribute to Charlie Parker, "Requiem." The trend-setting pianist layers his solos against himself, suggesting a procedure which later became identified with Bill Evans. Tristano also foreshadowed the fast, toccata-like lines in the piano's tenor range so celebrated in Evans's middle-period playing.

Tristano's nightclub appearances were understandably sporadic. Critics were merciless with him for being too cerebral. A heart attack ended a career with few parallels in jazz for controversy and misunderstanding.

Photo: Frank Driggs Collection

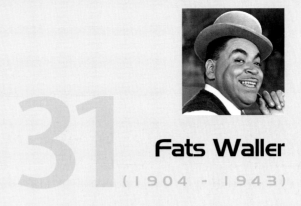

31 Fats Waller

(1904 - 1943)

Thomas "Fats" Wright Waller played, wrote, and sang some of the happiest music in the history of jazz. His rollicking style, flair for comic banter, and visual antics barely disguised an uncommonly creative force. Listeners in the millions for whom relentless *Sturm und Drang* are, fortunately, not prerequisites for jazz genius, warmly received him. Waller's popularity was only exceeded by Louis Armstrong.

Waller's precocious talent as a child led to the purchase of a family piano. There was no dearth of local piano teachers in his native Harlem when he began lessons with a Miss Perry. His studies continued in his mid-teens with the coaching of James P. Johnson. One of the founders of stride, Johnson helped to rescue ragtime's oompah and rigid syncopation from formulaic predictability. The elder pianist freely shared stride's trade secrets with his protégé. His knowledge of classical music played a vital role in developing Waller's considerable "chops."

A quick study, Waller was soon participating in cutting contests—competitions with the aura of a heavyweight championship fight, among a bevy of pianists trying to best each other in any key and at any tempo. Waller also met the demanding requirements for providing music at rent parties. The rent party was a unique Harlem solution to the problem of satisfying a rent deficit; the host/tenant simply charged admission to a gathering of hell-raisers. For a pianist, these could be grueling marathons lasting as long as ten or twelve hours. The high-energy stride, spontaneous creativity, and quick verbal wit of Johnson's star pupil made him a fixture on the circuit. His mastery of jazz organ (its first practitioner) deserves an accounting beyond the scope of this book.

Waller's first important solo piano recordings (1929, originally on RCA Victor, now reissued on Jazz Chronological Classics) established his pre-eminence in the stride movement. He surpassed the sly Willie "The Lion" Smith and even Johnson in all the essentials of the one-man-band style. The mighty swing, control of dynamics, and weapons-grade technique of Waller at his peak were impressive by any style's yardstick and very influential. Art Tatum, Erroll Garner, Mary Lou Williams, and particularly Count Basie channeled him often enough to qualify them as "Waller-ites."

By the mid '30s, the zany asides he often added on the hundreds of records he made as the singer/pianist/leader of Fats Waller and His Rhythm proved to be a mixed blessing. The spotlight increasingly shone on his capacity to entertain, and his piano playing was reduced to a secondary novelty.

Waller wrote successful Broadway shows, appeared in two films (*Hooray for Love* and *Stormy Weather*) and four "soundies" (forerunners of today's rock videos); but wealth and celebrity afforded him little personal fulfillment. His *London Suite*, a set of five reflective piano miniatures recorded in England in '39, indicates what might have been, had gargantuan drinking and eating habits not contributed to the shortening of his life. His other numberless compositions include "Ain't Misbehavin'," "Honeysuckle Rose," and "I've Got a Feeling I'm Falling."

Photo: Alan Nahigian

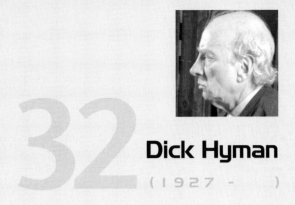

32 Dick Hyman

(1927 -)

A native New Yorker, Dick Hyman was attending Columbia University when he

entered a radio jazz piano contest. The radio exposure spearheaded his career. As

the contest's winner, he was granted a dozen free lessons with one of his idols,

Teddy Wilson.

The venerable Wilson noted Hyman's already exceptional technique, and continued to develop it by recommending Chopin's finger-busting études for practice material. In the mid '90s, Wilson's star pupil gave an affectionate nod to his former teacher by incorporating Wilsonian harmony and trademark pianistics throughout his arrangement of "If I Had You" for Woody Allen's film musical, *Everyone Says I Love You*.

Hyman is a musical chameleon, with the uncanny capacity to reproduce any style, from ragtime to the avant-garde. He has been called upon, perhaps too often, to channel Scott Joplin, Fats Waller, James P. Johnson, Willie "The Lion" Smith, and Duke Ellington for lecture/recitals and recordings. Such ventures, when further burdened by the demands of an active schedule as an arranger and a pedagogue, proscribe the time needed to define a voice of one's own. Even when freed from the strictures of a re-creation project (*Live at Café des Capains*, Music & Arts, 1989), the pianist swings effortlessly, as usual, in an appealing composite of Fats Waller, Art Tatum, and Wilson's styles; but the real Dick Hyman remains a phantom without a calling card.

As a young gun on the late-'40s New York jazz scene, Hyman became house pianist at the newly opened Birdland. He also worked with Red Norvo (1949–50), and toured Europe with Benny Goodman (1950). When an MGM recording contract yielded his piano trio hit single, "Moriate" (1956), Hyman was suddenly converted into commercial hot property. Throughout the late '50s and early '60s, he arranged and played ragtime solos on recordings as the infamous Knuckles O'Toole, played organ for soap operas and the TV game show "Beat the Clock," and served as Arthur Godfrey's musical director at CBS. One of the first musicians to explore the potential of electronic instruments, he played the Moog (an early edition of the synthesizer) on Enoch Light's Command label.

Hyman reactivated his jazz career in the late '60s, appearing at Dick Gibson's prestigious Colorado Jazz Parties, Eddie Condon's club, and the Newport Jazz Festival of '72. A series of recordings followed, not the least of which was a session with Lee Wiley (CD on Audiophile) that features the eclectic pianist in top form. Highly competitive, Hyman has played duets and recorded with Roger Kellaway and Derek Smith. Pairings with the latter (*Dick and Derek at the Movies*, Arbors Records, 1998) showcase an especially relaxed kindred-spirit vibe.

Hyman is still in demand to wear many hats. He has scored several Woody Allen films, published folios of his compositions and transcriptions, and remains artistic director for the Jazz in July series held annually at the 92nd Street "Y" in New York City.

Photo: Lee Tanner/Jazz Image

33 Wynton Kelly
(1931 - 1971)

Wynton Kelly shares a West Indian heritage with Oscar Peterson and Monty

Alexander. Jamaican-born, but raised in Brooklyn, New York from the age of four,

Kelly had no more than a negligible musical education. His experience in rhythm

and blues bands as early as 1943 (when he was twelve years old), was demonstra-

bly useful in the acquittal of his duties, toward the end of the decade, with such

blues-based employers as Lockjaw Davis and Dinah Washington. He was then, and

remained, Washington's favorite accompanist. The self-appointed "Queen of the

Blues" hired him, when availability permitted, for a total of three years.

Being an exemplary accompanist for vocalists and a valued sideman for instru-mentalists (Dizzy Gillespie, Lester Young, Charles Mingus), temporarily stalled Kelly's career as a soloist. The handful of recordings he led on Blue Note, Riverside, and Milestone were overshadowed by his grunt work, through most of the '50s, for leaders whose star power, of necessity, limited his solo space. In 1957, he com-pletely relinquished the spotlight as a pianist by playing bass—a skill he picked up during a hitch in the Army—on a recording session for vocalist Abbey Lincoln.

It remained for Miles Davis to rescue Kelly from near oblivion. Their long associa-tion began rockily, but ended well. The pianist was befuddled to find Bill Evans in attendance for the 1959 record date which produced Davis's landmark *Kind of Blue* album. Evans had left Davis some months before the session, and from all appear-ances, was reclaiming the piano bench. Kelly, called upon to play on only "Freddie Freeloader" (the one "grounded" entry on the album's otherwise gravity-free, modal universe), was relieved to discover that there were no plans to use Evans after the session. Davis had simply seen no conflict in hiring both pianists to ren-der their individual areas of expertise. Kelly was urged to stay on as the group's reg-ular pianist, and did so. His rhythm-section teammates—bassist Paul Chambers and drummer Jimmy Cobb—joined Kelly when he left in 1963. Five years in one of the most popular and revered groups in jazz had finally made his solo career possible.

Kelly's relaxed yet exuberant style was in full flower by the mid '60s. With increasing opportunities to choose his own repertoire, he played show tunes, jazz heads, and neglected gems like "Old Folks." In spite of Charlie Parker's famous recording of the unusual ballad, it never caught on with jazz's many flightless "Birds." Sparked particularly by Cobb's inventive drumming, Kelly's groove-oriented performances reached a large audience. Some of his best work has been reissued on Original Jazz Classics; and *Smokin' at the Half Note* (Verve), featuring guitarist Wes Montgomery, never dampens the album title's expectations.

Considering his limited training, Kelly was a good technician. While his above-mentioned West Indian brethren, Oscar Peterson and Monty Alexander, surpassed him in sheer chopsmanship, all three pianists were equals as wholesalers of cheerful, sun-drenched playing. In a perfect world, Kelly would not have suffered the epileptic seizure that prematurely took his life at the age of 40 in a Toronto motel.

Photo: Alan Nahigian

34 Dave McKenna

(1930 -)

Dave McKenna's playing has delighted many of his peers. George Shearing, Dick Hyman, Roland Hanna, and Bobby Hackett are only a few of his fellow musician admirers. Hackett, without blinking, called him "the greatest piano player alive." Yet, McKenna, an independently minded New Englander from Woonsocket, Rhode Island, is inclined to resist the classification "jazz musician." Modest in the extreme, he is uneasy over any praise of his work. When pressed to the wall, he prefers to be called a "barroom piano player." If a barroom repertoire is defined by a cornucopia of theater and Tin Pan Alley composers, with a noticeable absence of bebop "heads," McKenna qualifies for the rubric.

McKenna joined the musicians' union at fifteen, subsequent to a short history as a half-hearted piano student of his mother and parochial school nuns. Once his career goal was set, he studied in earnest with Sandy Sandiford and A. Peloquin. At sixteen, he played showers and weddings with a small group led by ex-Kenton altoist Boots Mussulli. He worked with Charlie Ventura in 1949 and Woody Herman in 1950 until he was drafted in 1951. Discharged in '53, McKenna rejoined Ventura briefly, and spent the rest of the '50s with Gene Krupa, Stan Getz, and a group co-led by Al Cohn and Zoot Sims. After some engagements with Buddy Rich in 1960, he divided his time between working with Bobby Hackett and appearances at Eddie Condon's in Manhattan's East Fifties.

New York City was McKenna's base of operations until he moved to Cape Cod in '67. Near-exclusive contact with New York mainstreamers changed McKenna's playing. Once a confirmed bebopper, he became a convert to the stylistic middle-ground of jazz, where, as Condon liked to say, "We don't flat our fifths—we drink 'em."

McKenna found himself encouragingly marketable as a solo pianist in and around the Cape. (Solo playing in the wrong room and, needless to say, the wrong hands, is as welcome as a hymn in a cathouse.) The reasons for McKenna's success as a one-man band then and now are obvious: the walking bass lines and guitar-like chord interpolations in the left hand, the hard-swinging right, the tasteful harmonic choices, and the endless backlog of great songs. His heroes are songwriters rather than jazz pianists—a fact which probably contributes to his self-disqualification from true jazz playing. Nonetheless, the ghost of Lennie Tristano haunts McKenna's recorded tributes to two of his favorite tunesmiths: *A Tribute to Hoagy Carmichael* and *Dancing in the Dark and Other Music of Arthur Schwartz* are both Concord CDs that were recorded in the early '80s.

McKenna's work begs comparison to other popular solo pianists. There is little linkage with Art Tatum, except that both pianists' repertoires sometimes overlap. In the case of Keith Jarrett (even the more recent, standards-centric Keith Jarrett), McKenna's mainstream conservatism rejects the more current trends in jazz, particularly in matters of harmony and rhythm.

Photo: Alan Nahigian

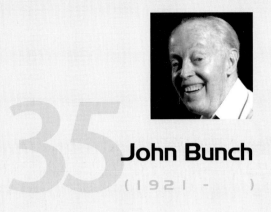

35 John Bunch

(1921 -)

Octogenarians are rare in jazz—the jazz life is high-maintenance; not designed for longevity. Those few musicians who survive middle age are often rewarded by declining creative powers and/or stylistic obsolescence. John Bunch, now well into the eighth decade of his life, has averted those pitfalls while doing what he has always done—assay well-crafted songs in tasteful, inventive ways. A committed mainstreamer, he makes no apologies for his allegiances to Teddy Wilson and Bud Powell. His fans are happy to note that his timeless playing is never threatened by the current flavor-of-the-month tyro.

The long Bunch odyssey began in Tipton, Indiana, where he played his first pro-fessional jobs at the age of twelve, after only two years of piano study. The jobs kept coming until the WWII draft. In 1944, on his seventeenth mission in the USAAF, Bunch was shot down over Germany. A POW for the remainder of the war, he was characteristically more disheartened by having to miss a Glenn Miller con-cert in London than he was by the other constraints of his Nazi hosts. The expe-rience lends added dimension to his *World War II Love Songs* (Lester, 2001). He attended the University of Indiana as a speech major (1946–50) before returning to active playing.

Bunch acquired extensive big band experience early on. There were stints with Woody Herman, Maynard Ferguson, Buddy Rich, and Benny Goodman—includ-ing the latter's tour of the USSR in '62. He remained fairly hidden in large ensem-bles until the '60s, when he began appearing at Eddie Condon's club and Luigi's in New York City. After touring with Tony Bennett as his accompanist and musical director (1966–72), he went back on the payrolls of Goodman and Rich. In '76, he became a member in very good standing of the swing revival group, the World's Greatest Jazz Band. Almost always cast in a supporting role, Bunch had yet to hit his stride as a soloist.

John's Bunch is Bunch's first recording session under his own name. Originally issued on Famous Door in '75 and reissued on Progressive in '02, it is a felicitous gathering of old friends. Sidemen Al Cohn, Urbie Green, Milt Hinton, and Mousey Alexander cover their tasks well, and the leader shows more of his bebop side than he had occasion to before. The session initiated a series of well-received Bunch recordings; good-natured, swinging dates with no pretensions to restless innovation.

Bunch made a smooth stylistic transition from Teddy Wilson to Bud Powell after the war. His ballads are still Wilsonian in their tasteful flourishes between phrases, and deft harmonic rhythm, although some listeners may miss the tender back stories Wilson used to tell. The Powell linkage, replete with Powell's occasional Monkish asides, shows at faster tempos without resorting to frayed clichés.

Bunch generally takes the road less traveled—even in his repertoire. The neglected bebop gems he chose to record on *A Special Alliance* (Arbors, 2002) may surprise those who think of him as primarily a swing pianist. The album includes Bunch's composition "Don't Remind Me"—previously heard in a white-noise Muzak arrangement in hotel elevators worldwide—which Bunch reclaimed as a gentle, appealing bossa nova.

Photo: Lee Tanner/Jazz Image

142

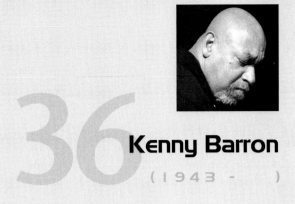

36 Kenny Barron
(1943 -)

The twain of old and new jazz traditions meet seamlessly in Kenny Barron's playing. A member of bebop's third generation, when the piano's reigning monarchs were Bud Powell, Horace Silver, and Red Garland, Barron has always kept abreast of the expanding frontiers of the music. He enjoys a good straight-ahead romp as much as the next mainstreamer, but he is also capable of a Tyner-esque, polyrhythmic meltdown when the occasion demands. In jazz piano circles, where versatility seldom rises above the level of appreciation afforded a favorite aunt's recipe for icebox cake, Barron's all-purpose capacities have always won him high praise. A valued educator (he has been a full-time instructor at Rutgers University since 1973), he brings the rich heritage of a veteran performing artist to the classroom.

Barron was born in Philadelphia. His piano lessons commenced at the age of six. From ages twelve through eighteen, he was a pupil of Ray Bryant's sister. He also studied bass and tuba while attending high school. In 1957, he played his first professional job with Mike Melvin's orchestra—a jazz-oriented R&B unit which included Barron's older brother, Bill, on tenor saxophone. Prior to moving to New York City in 1961, he worked with Philly Joe Jones and Jimmy Heath.

In the '60s and '70s, Barron was recruited by Dizzy Gillespie (1962–66), Freddie Hubbard (1966–70), Yusef Lateef (1970–75), and Ron Carter (1976–80). James Moody, Roy Haynes, Stanley Turrentine, and Lee Morgan complete a 20-year-long panoply of post-bop employers on his résumé. In 1980, Barron and Charlie Rouse co-founded Sphere, a popular quartet devoted to the music of Thelonious Monk. Sphere disbanded in 1986. The pianist has continually distinguished himself as a trio leader and soloist since he first recorded under his own name, but his participation in Stan Getz's valedictory recording *People Time* (Emarcy, 1991) is a reminder of his uncanny intuition as an accompanist.

Barron's style is unhurried and self-possessed. His solos have an arc with a purposeful ascent and descent in the best tradition of dramatically sound improvisation. He brooks none of the fashionable gospel licks of the neo-cons, yet tells a compellingly "sanctified" story. His single-note lines suggest the long-limbed grace of Tommy

Flanagan. Barron is at his best in the role of a collaborative artist. Interplay with another creative soloist—particularly one with enough of an opposing aesthetic to spark a degree of contention—brings out the risk-taker hidden in his trio and solo performances. His encounters with vibist Joe Locke, for example, on *But Beautiful* (Steeplechase, 1994), unleash enough of Barron's post-McCoy Tyner quirks to make something memorable out of what could have been merely a relaxed set of standards; while his duo recordings with Tommy Flanagan (an admitted idol) are too like-minded to be more than pleasantly routine.

Barron meets the challenges of teaching, performing, and composing ("Voyage" and "Phantoms" are well-traveled compositions) with admirable equanimity. It will be interesting to hear where the explorations of electronic music he began in the mid '90s will take him.

37

Bobby Timmons
(1935 - 1974)

In the late '50s and '60s, hard bop (or soul jazz) brought many new fans to jazz who would not otherwise have been recruitable at gunpoint. The style married bebop with gutsy gospel and blues-soaked elements. Driven by a shameless backbeat, it thumbed its nose at cerebral sophistication and directly addressed the libido. The demand for this music was ardently met by three North Philadelphia musicians—Lee Morgan, Benny Golson, and Bobby Timmons. Each played the style to a fare-thee-well and composed popular anthems for it. Timmons, however, eclipsed the others as a composer with "Moanin'," a catchy tune whose frequent airplay and chartbusting record sales were almost unprecedented in jazz. When the critics began performing post-mortems on hard bop (circa '65), Morgan and Golson found celebrity in other "bags" as players and composers, while Timmons's efforts to do the same went maddeningly unnoticed. Always an inventive musician, he resented the brush-off, lifelong.

Timmons's short and not always happy career began at the age of six with piano lessons from his uncle. Compromised by the usual childhood diversions, he later pursued instruction in greater depth during a year's attendance at the Philadelphia Musical Academy. His piano training overall remained spotty, and he never studied composition. A self-taught organist, Timmons often played for services at his pastor-grandfather's church. Like his soulful brethren—Gene Harris, Horace Silver, Hampton Hawes, and fellow Philadelphian Ray Bryant—Timmons was deeply affected by the music of the black sanctified church.

Timmons played his first jobs as a professional pianist with a local teenage dance band led by Lee Morgan. In 1956, he signed on with Kenny Dorham's Jazz Prophets. He joined Chet Baker in 1957 when it was decided that Baker's West Coast group needed an East Coast makeover. During Timmons's year among Art Blakey's hard boppers (1958–59), he wrote "Moanin'" for the biggest selling record Blakey ever made (*Moanin'*, Blue Note). Pen in hand again, he crafted two more hits—"Dis Here" and "Dat Dere"—while working with Cannonball Adderley's quintet (1959–60). Following another Blakey stint (this one brief), he led his own trio on the New York club circuit.

Only a modest success as a soloist/leader, Timmons failed to bank the fires he started as a tunesmith. His straightforward, swinging piano solos were no more appreciated than when they were buried under the carpet-bombing drummers of his hard bop days. The unfulfilled promise of this talented artist is not easily explained. Audibility was no longer Timmons's problem. Nor had his gift for writing attractive themes shown any decline. Perhaps he is a casualty of the average jazz fan's inability to juggle more than eight or ten artists at a time. Perhaps there were too many pianists in the '60s and early '70s who served up Timmons's Bud Powell, Red Garland, and Wynton Kelly cocktail—although few did it as unselfconsciously as he did. Maybe he should have retained (à la Horace Silver) the two-horn front line of his popular tunes. In any case, *From the Bottom* (Original Jazz Classics, 1964) and *Workin' Out* (Prestige, 1966), make for rewarding listening.

His career in a tailspin, Timmons was drawn into the powerful vortex of alcohol abuse. He died at 38 of cirrhosis of the liver.

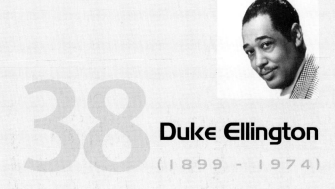

38 Duke Ellington
(1899 - 1974)

Some have accused Edward Kennedy "Duke" Ellington of cribbing melodic ideas from his sidemen for his most successful songs. Portions of and/or entire scores published under his name are rumored to be the work of his writing associate Billy Strayhorn. Ellington's piano playing, it seems, is the only area of his creative output that can lay claim to incontestable authorship. His career as a composer and the leader of one of jazz's great orchestras for nearly 50 years is well documented elsewhere. It is Ellington the pianist who concerns us here.

The child of black bourgeoisie parents in Washington, D.C., Ellington had all the cultural advantages of a middle-class background. At first, exposure to light classical music, operatic arias, and sentimental songs proved to be of little interest to him. Piano lessons with Marietta Clinkscales, a local teacher, began and ended quickly. A more serious musical bent surfaced in his early teens with his first efforts at composition: trifles in the popular ragtime style of the day. He formed a close friendship with Henry Grant, a schooled musician who directed the band at Ellington's high school. Grant gave the youngster some useful tips on harmony and piano playing and encouraged his bourgeoning interest in becoming a professional musician. A degree of success in regional dance bands finally determined Ellington's commitment to a career in music.

In the spring of '23, he set out for New York, finding himself in a city boiling over with good piano players out of work. Momentarily discouraged, he left, but returned in the fall with Elmer Snowden's Washingtonians. In '27, Ellington made his bones with an expanded edition of the Washingtonians under his leadership during an historic engagement at the Cotton Club.

Once he discovered that his true passion was writing (composing for the Cotton Club's spectacular floorshows sparked it), Ellington reduced the piano to an avocation. It follows that only small doses of his ear-tweaking solos can be found in an otherwise vast recorded legacy.

The Ellington piano style is as easily recognizable as the styles of Earl Hines, Art Tatum, or Bud Powell. Allowing for an occasional "Willie Smithism" (the legacy of a long friendship with "The Lion" of stride piano), it is virtually *sui generis*. There are inherent melodic and harmonic elements that mirror the adventurous orchestration of the composer's "Warm Valley." Parallels with Thelonious Monk, whom he clearly influenced, can be drawn. Neither had more than a haphazard musical education nor developed a virtuoso technique. Each was fond of rhythmic displacement, dissonant chord clusters, Bermuda Triangle chord sequences, and a kind of playful *gravitas*, where the serious somehow meets the absurd without contradiction. Pianists Randy Weston and Cecil Taylor also borrowed Ellingtonia.

In '62, *Money Jungle* (Blue Note), one of Ellington's rare outings as a trio pianist, puts him in the fast company of bassist Charles Mingus and drummer Max Roach. A quartet recording with John Coltrane (on Impulse) appeared in the same year. The sessions highlight a singular Ducal virtue—timelessness. He was on the cutting edge of the styles of the day well after critics were performing postmortems on swing and bebop. Even in his last years, Ellington the pianist amazed many a young turk and not a few old ones.

Photo: Frank Driggs Collection

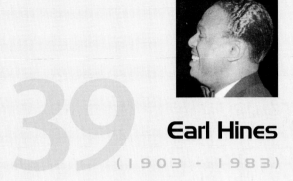

39 Earl Hines

(1903 - 1983)

Earl Hines's late-'20s recordings with Louis Armstrong's Hot Five and Hot Seven raised the curtain on the jazz piano styles of the future. His so-called "trumpet style" octaves in the piano's upper register, laced with sassy, knotted runs and unpredictable left-hand antics, doomed ragtime and early stride styles to obsolescence. The influence of "Fatha" (an apt sobriquet for the progenitor of such descendants as Art Tatum, Teddy Wilson, Nat "King" Cole, Mary Lou Williams, and Erroll Garner) persisted through bebop and continues to the present day.

Hines was born to musician parents in Duquesne, Pennsylvania, a suburb of Pittsburgh. His mother was his first piano teacher. Later, private tutors exposed him to the classics. He was not to dawdle long in local bands; singer Lois Deppe hired him for a tour in '23. By '27, he was working with Louis Armstrong's Chicago Stompers in the Windy City. Hines and Armstrong had formed a warm, enduring friendship before they recorded the seminal Hot Five and Hot Seven sessions of '28. The pianist is Satchmo's only equal in the ensembles—a fact made particularly clear on "Weather Bird Rag," one of several duets among their nineteen sides.

His mature style, firmly in place, Hines led a first-rate big band from 1928–40 at Chicago's Grand Terrace, one of the city's top nighteries. The band's twenty-year history ended in '48—a victim of an entertainment tax and fewer and fewer bookings in theaters and ballrooms. Some of its stellar alumni bear witness to the leader's flair as a talent scout. They include: Trummy Young, Freddy Webster, Budd Johnson, Bennie Green, Charlie Parker, Dizzy Gillespie, Wardell Gray, and vocalists Billy Eckstine and Sarah Vaughan.

Joining Armstrong's All-Stars (1948–51) helped set Hines's table but did little else for an artist who had long outgrown the confines of Dixieland. He languished in relative obscurity, fronting small groups and running a short-lived nightclub, until three critically acclaimed concerts at the Little Theater in New York City in 1963 revived his career. The return to the spotlight precipitated an avalanche of requests for his services at clubs, festivals, and recording sessions. Many of the latter were produced by British jazz critic Stanley Dance.

Hines sustained a high level of creativity until the end of his life. Even the arthritis and heart problems of his last years could not throttle the powerful beat and free-wheeling imagination he revealed on his recorded tributes to Duke Ellington and Cole Porter (New World Records). Each songsmith is afforded the tender mercies only a gifted composer/pianist can provide (Hines, after all, wrote the well-traveled jazz anthem "Rosetta").

Fatha's closest matches for sheer exuberance in the jazz piano pantheon are Fats Waller and Erroll Garner.

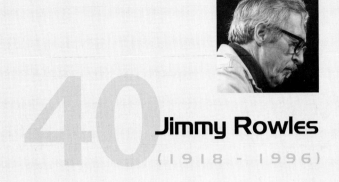

40 Jimmy Rowles

(1918 - 1996)

Jimmy Rowles hailed from Spokane, Washington. At a tender age, he began to imitate the piano ramblings of his mother, who played by ear. His later passion for tennis made him, at best, a bemused piano student with a number of short-term teachers—until he heard Teddy Wilson. Racquets and backhands were no more than a dim memory as Rowles, strutting his best Wilson impression, claimed the piano bench in the bands of Bob Crosby, Benny Goodman, and Woody Herman.

With the attrition of big bands after WWII, Rowles focused on small group work with Lester Young, Charlie Parker, Ben Webster, and Zoot Sims in and around Los Angeles, his new home. A series of engagements and recordings with Billie Holiday launched a brilliant, if low profile, career as an accompanist with almost every major singer in the business. Years later, he would reflect on his experiences with Holiday as the most memorable of all his vocal associations: "You had to love her. Too much chick."

Rowles's versatility affected a profitable career (and further anonymity) in Hollywood film studios. He plays the boogie-woogie calliope part on Henry Mancini's "Baby Elephant Walk" for *Hatari*, and appears on several other Mancini soundtracks throughout the '50s and '60s. The Hollywood years also bore some peripheral fruit: anyone who has heard Rowles's croaky, but musician-like, vocals will not be surprised to know that he was Marilyn Monroe's singing coach for a picture. When the great synth invasion swept Hollywood—replacing studio musicians—he folded up his tent and headed for New York.

Rowles's participation in the 1973 edition of the Newport Jazz Festival rescued him from obscurity. He recorded often and well in New York. For the Columbia CD *Stan Getz Presents Jimmy Rowles: The Peacocks* (1975), he wrote "The Peacocks," a little masterpiece. *On We Could Make Such Beautiful Music Together* (Xanadu, 1978), his refreshing, unclassifiable playing particularly makes its mark.

Rowles is not a scorched-earth swinger, à la Oscar Peterson, nor does he try to be. Infectious grooves, however, tendered on bossas, middle tempos, and ballads are common. Teddy Wilson's influence remains only in occasional sequences of walking tenths. New models have emerged: a percussive, Ellingtonian attack and Garner's tendency to play slightly behind the beat. The relaxed wit (look out for quotes from Elgar to Ellington), cliffhanger phrases, and sudden outbursts of dense chords fairly splattered at forte levels are Rowles's own. His abstract style is sometimes misspent on long-forgotten songs; few listeners know them well enough to appreciate his imaginative reconstructions.

Rowles returned to California in the mid '80s. Poor health gradually restricted his work schedule. Toward the end, he occasionally appeared with his daughter, Stacy, a gifted trumpet and flugelhorn player.

Photo: Frank Driggs Collection

162

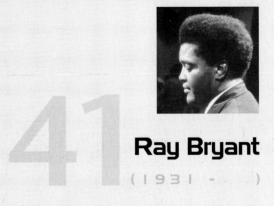

41 Ray Bryant
(1931 -)

Philadelphia-born Ray Bryant comes from a family of musicians. His mother and sister are accomplished gospel pianists and organists, his older brother Tommy, a bassist, played with many jazz greats, and his nephews include the talented Eubanks brothers, Kevin and Robin. Bryant's piano studies began at the age of eight and continued for the next eight years. He took theory lessons with the guitarist and banjoist Elmer Snowden, one of Duke Ellington's early Washingtonians, and learned to play bebop from listening to Red Garland in various neighborhood clubs. (Garland was a local resident in the jazz-volatile Philadelphia of Bryant's youth.) The budding musician was also affected by gospel music, the blues, Art Tatum, Teddy Wilson, and Bud Powell. As a result, a characteristic feature of his mature style began to emerge—the delicate balance of the old and the new.

41

Bryant gained valuable experience touring with Tiny Grimes (1948–49). After a freelancing period, he settled in as house pianist at two major Philadelphia jazz clubs: Billy Kretchmer's (1951–53) and the Blue Note (1953–56). In 1956, he joined Carmen McRae. He played for her Newport Jazz Festival appearance in 1957. In 1959, he returned to the festival as a member of the Jo Jones trio. Bryant's composition "Little Susie," an enormous hit single that he recorded in 1960, temporarily branded him as a "soul jazz" composer in spite of such earlier efforts as "Changes" and "Cubano Chant," which had addressed less fashionable trends. Bryant followed the money with a string of minor hits until 1962 when he demonstrated his versatility by recording with Elmer Snowden's sextet, Benny Carter, and Zoot Sims.

The mid '60s through the early '70s were a fallow period for musicians like Bryant, who not only questioned the propriety of the fusion style, but also refused to record covers of Beatles tunes. In 1972, Bryant rose like a jazz phoenix from the ashes of a near flat-lined career a more compelling artist than ever. Choosing the dicey context of unaccompanied solo playing, he asserted his return to the scene with a fine set of blues and standards on the stage of the Montreux Jazz Festival. The event is captured on *Alone at Montreux* (Atlantic). Thereafter, he resumed an active schedule as a popular trio leader and continues to do so, although his American engagements and recordings are all too rare of late. On *Tribute to His Jazz*

Piano Friends (JVC, 1997), he plays "Moanin'" in recognition of its composer Bobby Timmons. Bryant, unlike Timmons, a fellow Philadelphian, was spared the stigma of earlier "soul jazz" hits by no more an indemnity than a roll of the dice.

Bryant shares Hank Jones's flair for playing confidently without a rhythm section. They are not sound-alikes, however. Each is engaging in ways of his own, while using the full range of the instrument from its *altissimo* register to its *basso profundo*. Both are never so riveting as when they play the blues. Masters of the down-home epigram, they can reduce the breadth of a novel to a Post-it note. Their sharpest division lies in matters of harmony where Jones, Bryant's junior by thirteen years, is surprisingly the more daring harmonist.

Photo: Alan Nahigian

166

42 Herbie Hancock

(1940 -   )

Herbie Hancock began piano lessons at the age of seven and ended them at twenty. He supplemented the lessons by transcribing Oscar Peterson and George Shearing solos. He also deconstructed Claire Fischer's ambitious Hi Lo arrangements and Robert Farnon's face-lifting orchestrations of old standards.

While attending Grinnell College in Iowa, Hancock switched his major from engineering to music and graduated with a degree in composition. In 1960, he returned to his native Chicago where he worked with Coleman Hawkins when the legendary tenor saxophonist used a local rhythm section for an appearance in the Windy City. In that same year, Donald Byrd's group came to town for a booking during a blizzard. The weather stranded Byrd's regular pianist. Hancock subbed perfectly and accepted the leader's offer to move to New York as a permanent member of the group.

Hancock was well received in New York. He worked with Byrd (until '63), Phil Woods, Oliver Nelson, and Eric Dolphy. Blue Note signed him for a series of recordings. *Takin' Off* (1962), his debut as a leader, is a generous sampling of the pianist's style at the time (a hybrid of Bill Evans and Wynton Kelly), and includes the first recording of his composition "Watermelon Man." A prequel to his later rhythm 'n' blues interests, the tune became a cash cow when Mongo Santamaria recorded it the following year.

In the summer of '63, Hancock joined one of the finest bands Miles Davis ever assembled, playing a vital role in cutting-edge, polyrhythmic teamwork with Tony Williams on drums and Ron Carter on bass. His intuitive accompanying skills were tested by frequent fly-by-the-seat-of-your-pants changes of tempo and mood. A repertoire of modal, open-ended compositions by Davis and Wayne Shorter forced Hancock to find a solution to the problem of soloing with almost limitless creative freedom, while tempering an undesirable component—self-indulgence. He found his own voice before leaving Davis in '68.

Hancock has become one of the most influential pianists of his generation. Less percussive than Chick Corea (whom Davis replaced him with) or McCoy Tyner, Hancock is closer to the lyrico-romantic musings of Keith Jarrett. Elements associated with modern European classical music inform his harmony without compromising a pronounced sense of the blues. His work has the mighty endorsement of Oscar Peterson, who should know whereof he speaks, having played a piano-duo concert tour with him in the '80s. A two-piano conversation is a happy medium for Hancock's synergistic talent as demonstrated on *An Evening with Herbie Hancock and Chick Corea* (Columbia, 1978).

Hancock's electronic pop period (1973–78) enraged the jazz elite, but the throbbing riffs and licks were inspired as much by an honest attraction to the music of Sly and the Family Stone as they were by avarice. His return to jazz appears to be permanent. In 1986, he received an Academy Award for his score for *'Round Midnight*, a film loosely based on the lives of Bud Powell and Lester Young.

43 Jelly Roll Morton

(1885 - 1941)

A braggart's braggart, Jelly Roll Morton has often been pilloried for his shameless self-promotion. In a letter to *Downbeat* magazine (circa 1938), he wrote, "I, myself, happened to be the creator of jazz in the year 1902." He was known to roll back the actual year of his birth to 1885 in the attempt to fortify the preposterous boast. Morton's biographers have drained most of the swamp of pure hokum surrounding their elusive subject, but an indisputably accurate reconstruction of Morton's life has yet to be written. Even the Library of Congress project, in which the pianist recorded his autobiography (eight LPs on Riverside, 1939) cannot be taken seriously as a definitive document.

Morton was born Ferdinand Joseph Lamothe in New Orleans, Louisiana. His parents divorced when he was still a child. Upon his mother's second marriage, he was given his stepfather's surname—Mouton. Distaste for his surrogate parent led to the youngster's later version of the appellation. And as for the scurrilous origins of his nickname—the less said, the better.

In the best cultural tradition of his Creole heritage, Morton was exposed to operas, art songs, and light concert music at an early age. He excelled at his classical piano studies. (Morton was a better technician than he is generally given credit for.) He was also attracted to ragtime pianists of the day like Tony Jackson. A Storyville fixture, Jackson was the only pianist Morton ever expressed an admiration for. The attention Jackson and other ragtimers got in the wild nightlife of the Big Easy was not lost on an already super-sized ego. After his own success in red-light district sporting houses, the pianist began an aimless, nomadic existence. He made piano rolls (many of which were studied by a young Mary Lou Williams) in major cities across the country; but until the 1920s, his musical pursuits were subordinate to other interests such as pool hustling, gambling, pimping, and entertaining in vaudeville.

In 1923, Morton moved to Chicago, where he was to make his greatest contribution to jazz. From 1926–27, as the pianist/leader/arranger of the Red Hot Peppers, he recorded seventeen sides with a septet and two with a trio (*Birth of the Hot*, RCA

Bluebird). All featured mostly his own compositions. The septet's personnel were handpicked by the leader, who carefully rehearsed the execution of his difficult arrangements. Models of the New Orleans tradition of lusty ensemble work, they also offer fine, high-spirited piano solos. The latter, though anchored in ragtime, swing with much greater freedom. Nimble passagework and a rocking left hand are discharged with a refreshingly gentle, unforced pianism. Breaks, a familiar Morton device, are frequent. Morton's solos make more stops than a cross-town bus.

His influence on other pianists is marginal, perhaps, but it is hard to imagine that Earl Hines, Chicago-based at the time of the Red Hot Peppers's recordings, was not aware of the activities of his peer. Both were rebels against the constraints of ragtime—constraints which Hines eventually broke ties with completely. Morton, the less focused musician of the two, gave up the struggle with the advent of swing in the '30s, and became a caricature of himself. Ironically, one of his early compositions, "King Porter Stomp" (1902), became a swing-era favorite.

Morton spent most of the rest of his life trying to collect royalties for his compositions. For all of his bravado, he had signed contracts with unscrupulous publishers through the years. He died in California, leaving behind his last compositions. Still unrecorded, they are described by his biographers as bold, modern, and unlike any he'd written before.

Photo: Frank Driggs Collection

44 **Al Haig**

(1924 - 1982)

Inspired by a live radio pickup, from New York's 52nd Street, of a group co-led by

Charlie Parker and Dizzy Gillespie, Al Haig traveled from Boston to the Apple to

offer his services as a willing apprentice in the cause of the new music called

"bebop." In jazz, a savvy accompanist who can also hit the ground running as a

soloist is a valuable asset. Haig distinguished himself enough in both departments

to become one of Charlie Parker's favorite pianists. Their numerous recordings

together confirm this.

Born in Newark, New Jersey, Haig studied piano and theory as a child. The harp studies of his college days are reflected in his tendency to arpeggiate chords on ballads. Haig maintained unimpeachable bebop credentials throughout his career without cribbing from Bud Powell. His voicings are brighter, and his phrases are more inclined to begin on the downbeat. Lacking Powell's firepower, Haig was not predisposed to roar through the chord changes, but offered the compensatory virtue of a thoughtful lyricism. Although both men spoke the language of bebop, Powell used the authoritative voice of a motivational speaker—Haig chose the compassionate tone of a crisis hotline counselor.

Haig appeared and recorded with many jazz giants, yet his career was fraught with periods of obscurity. Other Caucasian pianists (George Wallington, Joe Albany, Dodo Marmarosa) suffered a similar fate in the black-dominated bop movement, and paid the rent by playing piano-bar gigs or working blue-collar jobs. Given the vicissitudes of the music business and Haig's outspoken opinions of other pianists, it is difficult to determine if the source of the problem was reverse discrimination or self-imposed exile.

Haig's almost psychic comping can be heard not only on classic recordings with Parker, but also with Stan Getz, Coleman Hawkins, Jimmy Raney (a personal friend), and Chet Baker. Miles Davis's groundbreaking *Birth of the Cool* sessions

(Capitol, 1948–50), include Haig on four outstanding tracks. An interesting, if somewhat restrained trio pianist, he is more volatile when sharing solo space in quartets or quintets. Haig plays electric piano with surprising flair on *Special Brew* (Spotlite, 1974), recorded in London. The solo piano recordings he made toward the end of his life occasionally reflected his days as a cocktail pianist working for wages in posh watering holes in Manhattan's Upper East Side.

Although Haig's influence has not been widespread, his cleanly executed, well-constructed solos are echoed in the styles of Bill Evans, Hank Jones, and Kenny Drew. Haig's support and encouragement during Drew's early days on 52nd Street are paid tribute in the latter pianist's less feral solos.

Photo: Alan Nahigian

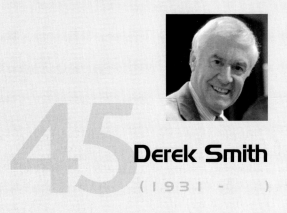

45 Derek Smith

(1931 -)

As his compatriot, George Shearing, had done a little more than a decade before,

Derek Smith left his native England in 1957, bound for permanent residence in

New York City. He had worked with the cream of British jazzdom, such as Johnny

Dankworth, and had also recorded for the BBC. The jazz opportunities at home

were fairly exhausted. Arriving in the Apple with no tangible prospects, he found

work as a solo pianist in Macy's sheet-music department. In short order, he was

chosen by John Lewis to represent the British faction of a recording project featur-

ing pianists from various countries. Smith seized the moment to demonstrate his

fine classical training and total command of the jazz language. His performance

green-lighted a successful Stateside career.

Smith has appeared and/or recorded with Benny Goodman, Clark Terry, and Tal Farlow, among many others. In 1967, he became a member of Doc Severenson's house band on the "Tonight Show," and remained until 1974, when Johnny Carson relocated the proceedings to Burbank, California. He toured Japan with Benny Carter in 1983. A remarkably versatile accompanist, Smith has provided insightful backdrops for styles ranging from Mel Tormé's "sighs-does-matter" approach to the jazz/pop warblings of Marlena Shaw. Forays into explicit pop include recordings with Dionne Warwick, and Steve Lawrence and Eydie Gorme.

Smith is an eclectic, at home in any of the jazz piano traditions that precede the avant-garde. He is frequently asked to play at Dick Gibson's Colorado jazz parties where pianists disinclined to "freak out" are always welcome. He uses his synthesis of the styles of Bud Powell and Oscar Peterson to good advantage on the piano duo album *Dick [Hyman] & Derek [Smith] at the Movies* (Arbor). Smith is, however, easily distinguished from Hyman: he is the more bop-oriented of the two. When the arrangements call for stride style, the Brit proves himself a worthy primo or secondo partner, as well. He walks a fine line between Teddy Wilson and early Bud Powell in bands led by neo-swingsters Scott Hamilton and Warren Vache; but, John Bunch, Smith's senior by ten years, is clearly more comfortable wandering through the boneyards of swing for an entire evening.

On his many recordings as a trio leader, he shows close affinities with his favorite pianist, Oscar Peterson. Smith is one of the few players with the technical equipment to express those affinities. *Derek Smith Plays Jerome Kern* (Progressive, 1980), a send-up to a composer who once held Smith's old job at Macy's, reveals a bluesy, fire-stoking swinger and logical improviser who could pass for O.P. were it not for the conservative "lick" patterns and tame harmonizations. *Love for Sale* (Progressive, 1976) is more personal, more risk-taking. For movie fans, a typical Smith hit-the-ground-running intro is heard under the opening titles of Woody Allen's *Crimes and Misdemeanors,* a film in which he also appears briefly as an extra in a nightclub scene. Other Allen soundtracks (*Hannah and Her Sisters, Radio Days, Everyone Says I Love You*) feature his solos and accompaniments. Smith still makes his home in New York.

Photo: Redferns Music Picture Library

46 Ralph Sharon

(1923 -)

Ralph Sharon knows more standards than a busload of Shriners. His knowledge was

accrued in nearly a half-century of service as accompanist and musical director for

several A-tier vocal interpreters of the *Great American Songbook*. His long history of

indenture with singers surpasses even that of Jimmy Rowles. Coupled with Sharon's

keen understanding of the machinery of Cole Porter, George Gershwin, Harold Arlen,

et al, is his grasp of another accompanist's essential—immediate access to whichev-

er chord, riff, or phrase of the moment will serve as the perfect *bon mot* for the story

the singer is telling. He is so whip-smart at the job that his schedule has rarely per-

mitted the opportunity to showcase his none-too-shabby wares as a soloist.

Born in London, England, Sharon studied piano with his mother, an excellent American pianist. He made his professional debut with Ted Heath's jazz-oriented dance band in 1946. Alternating with George Shearing, he appeared on trumpeter Kenny Baker's popular BBC radio broadcasts of "Baker's Dozen," and also worked with tenor saxophonist Ronnie Scott ('48). Sharon ended the '40s leading a sextet at London's fashionable Stork Club, which included a teenage Victor Feldman on drums. In 1953, after winning four consecutive polls in England's *Melody Maker* magazine, Sharon headed for the American "colonies." (In 1947, George Shearing spearheaded such emigration, and Derek Smith followed Sharon in 1957. The three musicians share only the common bond of being British expatriates—their piano styles could not be more dissimilar.)

By the mid '50s, Sharon rated first-call status for recording sessions on the singer-friendly Bethlehem label. He frequently lent his services as pianist/arranger on many recordings with such Bethlehem vocal artists as Johnny Hartman, Chris Connor, and Mel Tormé. The die of a career accompanist was cast.

Shortly before he joined Tony Bennett in 1956, the pianist released his own LP (*The Ralph Sharon Trio*, Bethlehem), a very listenable mating of Teddy Wilson's feathery touch with Bud Powell's mercurial harmony. The association with Bennett lasted until 1968. A second pairing with the popular tenor began in 1980 (the years in between were spent as the power behind the thrones of Peggy Lee, Robert Goulet, and Rosemary Clooney), and ended in the late '90s with the announcement of Sharon's semi-retirement.

Sharon is now exclusively a solo recording artist. He continues to add to the series of blue-chip songwriter tributes that he began in 1991 with *The Ralph Sharon Trio Plays the Sammy Cahn Songbook* (DRG). Baritone saxophonist Gerry Mulligan is a special guest on the session. The songbooks of Jerome Kern, Irving Berlin, George Gershwin, and Richard Rogers have appeared as recently as 2001. Sharon's beat still gently rocks, and his harmony these days is lightly dusted with Bill Evans-ish voicings.

Mary Lou Williams
(1910 - 1981)

Mary Lou Williams's allure is near palpable in her early publicity headshots. It almost seems possible to smell her fragrance. The images are misleading. They suggest that the fetching young black woman with the hooded eyes and prominent cheekbones is likely a movie star, not a jazz pianist—let alone an extraordinary one. That she fared so well in those patriarchical "good ol' boy" days of jazz, in spite of her beauty and gender, is a testimony to her talent. She cleared the way for Marian MacPartland, Barbara Carroll, Eliane Elias, and many others to take their place at an honored table that had once been reserved only for female singers.

As a child, Williams spent endless hours at the player piano in her Pittsburgh home, dissecting the rolls of Jelly Roll Morton and James P. Johnson. Self-instruction was to remain the learning method of choice for her playing, arranging, and composing. She never had a formal lesson.

At age nineteen, already a veteran of gin joints and vaudeville, she joined a band led by her future husband John Williams. Her long tenure with Andy Kirk and the Clouds of Joy (1931–42) as featured soloist and principal arranger, launched her reputation as a musician's musician.

Briefly in '42, Williams formed a small group with her second husband, trumpeter Harold "Shorty" Baker. An ardent champion of bebop from the very beginning, she informally tutored Thelonious Monk and Bud Powell. Jam sessions were encouraged in her Harlem apartment. Erroll Garner, a fellow-Pittsburgher just beginning to attract attention on 52nd Street, often lent his party-hearty style to the proceedings. The jazz "salon" at 63 Hamilton Terrace frequently served as an annex of Minton's, the uptown nightclub where the bop revolution was born.

By the mid '40s, the former Queen of Boogie-Woogie (a one-dimensional rubric Williams always resented) defied pianistic classification. Her Hines-like cat-and-mouse games with time (a transcriber's nightmare), swinging Kansas City beat, and bop-infused harmony appealingly converged on a series of recordings for the

Asch, Bluebird, and Mercury labels. In '45, she premiered the "Zodiac Suite" for chamber orchestra, the first of her many extended-form compositions.

The years 1952–54 were spent among friends and other expatriate musicians in Europe, where her growing discontent with the venality of the music business and what she called the "frozen sounds" of younger players peaked. She returned to New York spiritually, as well as financially, bankrupt. Regenerated by a conversion to Catholicism in 1957, she ended a three-year semi-retirement by appearing with Dizzy Gillespie's big band at Newport (CD on Verve). Her playing was still fresh, and the critics responded with fulsome praise.

Williams's remaining years were very active: she busied herself with "Mary Lou's Mass" (a composition commissioned by the Vatican), teaching at Duke University, recording, and tending a thrift shop whose proceeds went to indigent musicians. In '77, her creativity was nonetheless worse for wear when she played piano duets in Carnegie Hall with the uncompromising nihilist Cecil Taylor.

She died of cancer in Durham, North Carolina. Her legacy continues under the watchful auspices of the Mary Lou Williams Foundation.

48

Willie "The Lion" Smith

(1925 -   )

In the early 1920s, a gaggle of Harlem piano players forged a style that liberated

ragtime from the starchy, monotonous genre it had become. The result, called

"stride," held the rag's basic template (an oompah in the left hand against synco-

pated figures in the right) to higher standards of melodic, harmonic, and rhyth-

mic sophistication. Willie "The Lion" Smith, along with James P. Johnson and Fats

Waller, were the superstriders of the movement.

Originally from Goshen, New York, Smith moved to Newark, New Jersey with his parents in 1911. He started piano lessons at an early age with his mother, a church organist. She was the only piano teacher he ever had. Drawn to show business, he danced for pennies in saloons. The piano rags he heard during an evening were diligently practiced at home. Gradually, his playing eclipsed his dancing career. An enlisted soldier in WWI, his heroic standoff (as he told it), firing a cannon on the front lines for 49 straight days, earned him the nickname "The Lion." It should be noted that Smith had a penchant for self-promotion.

In the 1920s, Smith threw his trademark derby hat in the highly competitive ring of Harlem "ticklers" where an ambidextrous, orchestra-in-itself style was a prerequisite for survival. He became an A-list player for clubs and rent parties (galas with an admission charged at the door of a tenant looking to make up the shortfall in rent). Perhaps his favorite métier was the cutting contest. On such an occasion, pianists with egos the size of yachts set about to metaphorically "cut" the house piano player. "The Lion," a cigar clenched between his teeth, would stand over a contender during an inept performance, delighted to ask, "When did you break your left arm?" Few had the temerity to continue and relinquished the bench. The master then proceeded to show them how it was "s'posed to be."

He worked mostly in New York City, except for three foreign tours: Europe during 1949–50, South Africa in '65, and Europe exclusively in '66. During the course of his long career, he had met and encouraged Mel Powell, Joe Bushkin, Artie Shaw, and the young Duke Ellington (who paid him a tribute in the composition "Portrait of a Lion").

In the '30s, Smith studied harmony, theory, and counterpoint, but lacked the classical piano training of his rivals Johnson and Waller. Smith, nonetheless, held his own as a technician, and he is often the most intriguing harmonist of the three. It is said that Art Tatum lent his considerable ears in the direction of the piano at Pod & Jerry's club where "The Lion's" chords often roared. Ellington felt that Tatum had incorporated what he called "Willie Smithisms" into his own style.

Smith's autobiography, *Music on My Mind* (Doubleday, 1964), with a foreword by Ellington, is a rich treasury of anecdote and humor. A series of his recordings for Commodore (1938 and '39) are now on CD (Jazz Chronological Classics). *The Memoirs of Willie The Lion Smith*, originally released on RCA in 1968, has been reissued on Koch Jazz.

Photo: Frank Driggs Collection

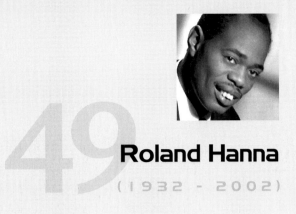

49 Roland Hanna

(1932 - 2002)

Roland Hanna, Tommy Flanagan, Hank Jones, and Barry Harris form the regional

collective known as the Detroit school. The youngest, and most academically

trained member of the group, Hanna had originally focused on classical music

until Flanagan introduced him to jazz. Adding Art Tatum and Bud Powell to his

classical allegiances, the converted pianist fashioned a style whose reconciliation

of the familiar with the unexpected came to be heard in the major cities of the

world. In 1970, Hanna relaxed a busy mega-mile itinerary long enough to be

knighted by the then-President of Liberia, William V.S. Tubman, for the outstand-

ing cultural and charitable services he rendered to that country. His distinguished

triple-threat career as pianist, composer, and teacher is not likely to be matched

in the foreseeable future.

Born in Detroit, Michigan, Hanna started private piano studies at the age of eleven with Ms. Josephine Love. Upon graduation from Cass Technical High School, he served a two-year hitch in the United States Army. Resuming his musical studies, he enrolled at the Eastman School of Music, and later at Julliard. He worked with Benny Goodman (1958), Charles Mingus (1959), Sarah Vaughan (1960–64, during which time he studied orchestration and conducting), and Carmen McRae (1965). Except for some solo concerts in Paris in 1968 and a television season in the house band of the "Dick Cavett Show" in 1973, Hanna could be found from the late '60s through the early '70s in the roaring Thad Jones/Mel Lewis orchestra at the Village Vanguard. He formed the New York Jazz Quartet in '75, and periodically joined forces with the ultimate mainstreamer, Zoot Sims, prior to his participation in the Lincoln Center Jazz Orchestra (1986–92). His last years were mainly devoted to composition (several extended-form works for orchestra, and a sonata for piano and violin) and teaching (as tenured professor at the Aaron Copland School of Music, Queens College, City University of New York).

For a musician accustomed to the discipline of serious composition, Hanna's improvisations are generally playful and unrestrained. His combustibility at the very outset of a solo—a virtue particularly useful in big-band work, when a few high-spirited piano choruses at the beginning of an arrangement can effectively launch a full ensemble tutti—was often pressed into service during his years with the Thad Jones/Mel Lewis orchestra. A master comper in all the big bands he played in, Hanna's accompaniment skills are in the brilliant, pro-active league of a Count Basie or a Duke Ellington.

Easy to Love (Koch, 1959), Hanna's first recording as a leader, is an embarrassment of bebop riches. True to his Detroit school credentials, he leans heavily on Bud Powell; but there are already traces of melodic and harmonic mediations from the French impressionists and Arnold Schoenberg's pre-twelve-tone period. The charm of Hanna's later work lies in how he forged traditional and more advanced idioms into a holistic narrative. On his *Live at Maybeck Recital Hall* (Concord, 1993), he occasionally sounds like his great friend Tommy Flanagan. Except for the courser tone and classical outsourcing, Flanagan might well have played some of the horn-like lines.

Hanna was an inspired teacher. His students include vocalist Dee Dee Bridgewater and the excellent Cuban pianist Alfredo Rodriguez.

Photo: Lee Tanner/Jazz Image

50 Keith Jarrett

(1945 -)

Keith Jarrett is Allentown, Pennsylvania's only significant jazz export. Proficient on several instruments (Stan Getz once tried to hire the teenage Jarrett on guitar), he started playing piano at the age of three. His extensive classical piano training was imparted by teachers assuming the heady responsibility of tutoring a prodigy. Self-taught as a composer, he declined a composition scholarship with Nadia Boulanger.

While attending Berklee College of Music in Boston in '62, he led a trio that served as the house rhythm section for Tony Scott and Roland Kirk on their visits to Bean Town. Though clearly gifted, Jarrett was, like many young pianists at the time, mainly a compendium of Bill Evans clichés. In '65, he aborted his Berklee studies and moved to Spanish Harlem in New York City. After a short hitch with Art Blakey, he joined Charles Lloyd's quartet (1966). Lloyd wisely mixed a palatable version of sixties avant-garde jazz with enough pop covers to attract a large following. During Jarrett's three-year tenure with the group, he rose from obscurity, sidestepped Evans's shadow, and blazed some trails of his own.

The '70s were vintage years for Jarrett. He signed on with Miles Davis (1970–71), reluctant, at first, to play electric keyboards. A recent fusion convert, Davis insisted that his pianists come to terms with such things. Jarrett ultimately "plugged in" out of sheer love of the leader's playing. He was rewarded by the high-profile exposure, but returned to acoustic music exclusively thereafter.

In 1972, Jarrett formed a quartet with saxophonist Dewey Redman, bassist Charlie Haden, and Paul Motian. The group's free-jazz interplay was surprisingly marketable. Jarrett's compositions provided good vehicles for his quirky improvisations. His playing achieved considerable transparency for all of its effusive lyricism, blizzards of single notes, and intense rhythmic activity. Jarrett, with the possible exception of Herbie Hancock, is alone among his peers in the search for textural lucidity.

The Koln Concert (ECM, 1974), began a numerically unprecedented series of solo jazz piano performances recorded live in the world's major concert halls. Jarrett's solo discography, by far, exceeds even Art Tatum's prodigious output. A typical sampling features his predilection for approaching music as a transcendental experience. New Age minimalism and gospel-tinged vamps abound, accompanied by Jarrett's audible sighs and foot-stomping. There are long, arid stretches suggestive of bleak landscapes—shattered, wind-tossed neon signs groan on their hinges in a ghost town; rock slags and giant trees with gnarled roots appear in a Jurassic tableau. This is not your father's bebop piano player.

Another Jarrett quartet incarnation (sometimes referred to as his European quartet) appeared in the late '70s, with Jan Garbarek on tenor and soprano saxophones, Palle Danielsen on bass, and Jon Christensen on drums. A more reflective unit than the previous American one, it produced the memorable *My Song* (ECM).

Since the mid '80s, the pianist has demonstrated a growing rapprochement with the past, recording standard songs (with bass and drums in a straight-ahead, head-solo-head format), solo works by Bach and Shostakovich, and several Mozart piano concertos.

20 The Next Twenty

Warren Bernhardt

Joe Bushkin

George Cables

Bill Charlap

Russ Freeman

Sanford Gold

Barry Harris

David Hazeltine

John Hicks

James P. Johnson

Pete Jolly

Lou Levy

John Lewis

Marian McPartland

Bill Mays

Mel Powell

Eric Reed

Richard Twardzik

Kenny Werner

Richard Wylands

Top Ten Women 10

Mary Lou Williams (1910 - 1981)

See #47 of The Top Fifty.

Marian McPartland (1918 -   )

The former Margaret Marian Turner from Slough, England, daughter of privilege-class parents, met Chicago-style cornetist Jimmy McPartland in Europe on the USO circuit during WWII. Their marriage in 1945 was the pianist's nose-thumbing response to social conventions and typical of her distain for predictability in any form. She had already shown a rebellious streak at the Guildhall School of Music in London. Her self-instruction, via recordings in the music of Duke Ellington, Sidney Bechet, and Teddy Wilson, were considered antithetical to the standard curriculum.

The McPartlands settled in Chicago in 1946. There she fell under the influence of Lennie Tristano's bold innovations. Tristano noted her unsteady beat in those days during an appraisal session. He suggested that she practice with a metronome, and her time vastly improved. By 1952, playing in her husband's Dixieland group became stylistically restrictive. The marriage had also proven to be an unhappy union, and McPartland moved to New York City.

Happier among the maverick beboppers on 52nd Street, she became a fixture at the Hickory House from '52–'60. Her enthusiastic playing and original harmonizations are captured on excellent live recordings (*At the Hickory House*, 1952–53, Savoy/Arista). Mainly a trio leader, except for a brief period with the Benny Goodman Sextet ('63), she has earned an estimable reputation through extensive recording, club and festival appearances, and her NPR series "Piano Jazz." The network's longest running program, "Piano Jazz" showcases McPartland's natural eclecticism in conversations and duets with pianists of every conceivable style. She celebrated her 80th birthday at a town hall concert with many guest artists in March of '98.

Eliane Elias (1960 -   )

One of the most creative expatriate musicians living in the United States, Eliane Elias is never far from her roots. The music of her Brazilian homeland is often synthesized with the American jazz of other artists, but rarely as seamlessly as she does it.

Elias was born on the southeastern coast of Brazil in the city of Sao Paulo. Her mother, a concert pianist, gave her piano lessons from an early age. Exposure to her mother's extensive jazz record collection motivated the precocious student to transcribe solos by Art Tatum, Bud Powell, Erroll Garner, and others before she was twelve. A professional by her mid-teens, Elias worked in every context—from big bands to solo gigs in restaurants. During a vacation in Paris, she met bassist Eddie Gomez, whose advice, after hearing her demo tape, was that she move to New York City. She bet the farm, arriving in Manhattan in 1981.

Her first important gigs were with the fusion group Steps Ahead. In 1983, she married its trumpeter, Randy Brecker. Before their troubled marriage led to a separation in the early '90s, Elias had become a successful trio leader and recording artist for Blue Note (*Plays Jobim*, 1989; glowing liner notes by Leonard Feather). Another session, now deleted, offered solo performances and some duets with savvy Brazilophile Herbie Hancock.

Elias has a mountain of technique. The influences of post-bop pianists Bill Evans, Chick Corea, and McCoy Tyner resonate in her work without self-conscious application. There are also references to Ahmad Jamal's octave tremolos and single-note, slightly behind-the-beat delineations on ballads. She will occasionally tamper with the formal structure of a standard: "Desafinado," for example, on *Plays Jobim*, ignores the bridge during the improvised choruses. The result can be convincing once you've accepted the modification. A small-voiced singer (Blossom Dearie, by contrast, is a loudmouth), Elias has mastered the peculiarly Brazilian art of converting shaky intonation into affecting vulnerability.

Jessica Williams (1948 -   )

Despite her voluminous discography (sixty LPs and CDs to date), Jessica Williams's playing remains a well-kept secret. And although her aversion to travel and a disinclination to micromanage the business aspects of her career go so far in explaining this problem, the jazz press has been derelict in its duty to marshal the troops on behalf of this *rara avis* among post-bop pianists.

Born in Baltimore, Maryland, Williams entered the Peabody Conservatory at the age of nine, leaving its hallowed halls at seventeen, already with a virtuoso technique. Her piano teacher, Richard Aitken, tailored her classical studies to complement her obvious skill at improvisation. Williams added to that a thorough investigation of the jazz piano canon.

In 1968, she moved to Philadelphia where she worked with Philly Joe Jones, Tyree Glenn, and played electronic keyboards (including the Hammond B3 organ) with local rock groups. A San Francisco resident since 1977, she gained some traction in the Bay Area by signing on as house pianist at Keystone Korner. Appearances with the eleven-piece Liberation Orchestra followed. She recorded for her own Quanta and Ear Art labels in the early '80s, playing synthesizer and over-dubbing herself on bass and drums. Borrowing from the collective consciousness of nearly every major jazz pianist living or dead, Williams had come upon a signature style by the mid '80s.

Her recordings for several small labels over the next two decades reveal an increasing affinity for near vocal communication; the declamatory phrasing she had pursued by now suggests actual speech patterns. A keen intelligence disallows for less than model continuity. On *Live at Yoshi's* (Max Jazz, 2004), one of her best recordings, her beautiful time allows for all manner of liberties with melody, harmony, and rhythm. Whatever is occasionally overwrought is redeemed by a playful sense of humor.

A follower of psychiatrist/philosopher William Reich, to whom she apparently feels indebted for her strongly communicative outreach, Williams has been the recipient of two NEA grants and a Guggenheim Fellowship.

Joanne Brackeen (1938 -   )

Joanne Brackeen claimed the piano bench with Art Blakey's testosterone-addled Jazz Messengers with characteristic pragmatism. She was in the audience when Blakey's pianist got lost on a tune. The performance was taking on water. She sat in, shone brightly, and won gainful employment as a reward. A pianist comfortable in her own skin, Brackeen has always sought practical solutions to creative problems. Equally pragmatic (some would say disengaged) about sexism in jazz, she notes in an interview for Linda Dahl's book, *Stormy Weather*, "I want a [bass] player at Eddie Gomez's level. What woman can I call?"

She was born Joanne Grogan in Ventura, California. Her natural ability as a child to reproduce Frankie Carle solos from her parents' record collection signaled an erratic history of formal piano study. She resisted classical training; her three days at the Los Angeles Conservatory of Music will live in infamy. Converted to jazz in her teens, Brackeen brought herself up to speed on bebop by self-instruction.

In 1960, while working and jamming on the L.A. club circuit with Dexter Gordon and Harold Land, she met saxophonist Charles Brackeen. Their marriage (they have since separated) yielded four children. The pianist retired to raise her family until the Blakey gig (1969–72). Joe Henderson, Sonny Stitt, and Stan Getz kept her busy through the remainder of the '70s. Recordings and festival appearances with her own units, often featuring bassists Cecil McBee or Eddie Gomez, have been earning well-deserved kudos since the '80s.

Brackeen's playing is impetuous. Her lines and rhythms pop off like strings of Chinese firecrackers (*Popsicle Illusion*, Arkadia, 1999). What there is of conscious deliberation is guided by post-Bill Evans stylistic parameters and occasional sly references to Charlie Parker. A major voice despite the neglect of the critics, Brackeen shares the fate of Jessica Williams as the elephant in the room.

Barbara Carroll (1925 -   )

A native of Worcester, Massachusetts, Barbara Carroll was a self-taught pianist from the age of five, until she began studies with a teacher at eight. She entered the New England Conservatory of Music in her late teens. Convinced that her interest in jazz was not sufficiently addressed there, she attended for only a year. While leading an all-girl trio for USO shows at Army camps in and around New England during the last days of WWII, she adopted a modified spelling of her middle name (Carole) as a surname (replacing Coppersmith). A post-war, mixed-gender edition of her trio, featuring Chuck Wayne on guitar and Clyde Lombardi on bass, was favorably reviewed in *Downbeat* magazine when the group played an engagement at the Downbeat Club in New York. In 1948, Carroll was Benny Goodman's choice (following his fall-out with Mary Lou Williams) to record with his short-lived bop combo, which featured Wardell Gray on tenor sax and other promising new blood.

By the early '50s, the "Carroll" style—a polished take on Bud Powell and Art Tatum—made for easy listening at the Embers in Gotham City. In 1953, the pianist took an acting/playing role in Rodgers and Hammerstein's Broadway success, *Me and Juliet*. Her trio recordings for Atlantic, RCA, and Verve at the time featured her bassist and husband Joe Shulman—a Claude Thornhill alumnus who had participated on Miles Davis's *Birth of Cool* sessions. Widowed in 1957, Carroll retired to raise a daughter.

A more insistent swinger than ever before since her comeback in 1976, she is also privy now to Bill Evans's additions to jazz's harmonic lexicon (*Everything I Love*, Cabaret DRG, 1996). Another element—the occasional vocal—has been added to her live appearances. (Upper Eastsiders, who frequent Bemelman's Bar, where Carroll worked from 1979 until recently, like to put a voice to the face of a solo pianist.) Carroll makes the concession better than most, and the results are, at least, "musicional." She appears briefly in a scene filmed on location at Bemelman's for Woody Allen's *Hollywood Ending*.

Dorothy Donegan (1922 - 1988)

Dorothy Donegan was a con. Her jokes, visual antics, and vocal impressions were a Trojan horse designed for easy access to fashionable supper clubs. Once within their walls, Donegan, draped in mink and blinking like a diamond-studded semaphore, began the slaughter of the innocents with her devastating piano virtuosity. A flamboyant figure, her response to Mary Lou Williams's criticism that she played too many runs, was typically ego-driven: "Some can and some can't. You don't play enough."

The Chicago native began piano lessons at the age of eight. Later studies at the Chicago Conservatory, the Chicago Music College, and the University of Southern California provided a solid bedrock of classical technique. Informally, Art Tatum was also her teacher and mentor. She launched her solo career at Costello's Grill in 1940. For her 1942 recording debut, she played two boogie-woogie solos, which were promptly released, and two classical pieces that were rejected. She continued to include works by Bach, Brahms, and Chopin in her repertoire, sometimes recasting them in the more palatable "swingin' the classics" mode. Donegan played a duo with Gene Rodgers in the film *Sensations of 1945*, and appeared on Broadway in the same year. There was a spate of New York recordings from 1946 to 1947, followed by sporadic recording activity.

Donegan sustained lengthy engagements at celebrated venues throughout her career, but many jazz lovers felt cheated by her vaudevillian side. Both predator and victim of her own shell game, she eventually lost a true jazz fanbase. Her live recording from Hank O'Neal's *Floating Jazz Cruise of 1992* (Chiaroscuro), reminds us that she was a serious artist at heart. In the best tradition of theme and variations, the pianist uses a melody as a trellis for garlands of decorative musical flora. There are more than a few nods here to Art Tatum, who often adopted the same approach to improvisation.

Forced to retire in the fall of '97 when she was diagnosed with cancer, Donegan sought treatment in Mexico. She died there in May of '98 after falling into a coma.

Lorraine Geller (1928 - 1958)

Lorraine Geller was an A-list pianist on the West Coast scene in the 1950s. Stylistically, she was perched on the seam of jazz piano tradition where Art Tatum meets Bud Powell, but not in thrall to either. Her long lines with their playful peek-a-boo phrases and judicious use of astringent intervals and harmonies were her own.

Born Lorraine Walsh in Portland, Oregon, her early piano training was rigidly classical until a progressive high school music teacher introduced her to jazz. Her first major exposure as a professional musician was with the International Sweethearts of Rhythm (1949–52), an all-girl ensemble in which she was affectionately nicknamed "Jazz" by her bandmates. A talented artist with pen and ink, Geller relieved the tedium of band bus travel between engagements by sketching portraits of such Sweethearts as trumpeter Norma Carson and bassist Bonnie Wetzel. She worked in a New York-based duo with Wetzel after the band broke up. In 1951, she married reedman Herb Geller. Before the end of 1952, the couple turned in their Local 802 cards and moved to Los Angeles.

The pianist thrived in the City of Angels. She appeared with all the luminaries of West Coast jazz, including Shorty Rogers, Maynard Ferguson, and Zoot Sims. In 1954, Geller and her husband formed a quartet many cuts above the typical horn-with-piano trio paradigm (*Herb Geller Plays*, reissued 2002, Universal CD). The group featured Mrs. Geller's close participation on the intricate "heads" and her deftly fingered solos. The Geller quartet continued to work and record until 1957, when its pianist, now an expectant mother, took maternity leave from playing.

The birth of a club-footed child put an emotional and financial strain on the Gellers. Lorraine, a lifelong asthmatic, prematurely returned to work as Kay Starr's accompanist to help pay the mounting orthopedic expenses, and developed pulmonary edema. On the morning of October 10, 1958, her heart stopped.

She accomplished a great deal in a life only thirty summers long—an early death, even by jazz standards of longevity. A spare but memorable recorded legacy refuses to reduce her to a historical footnote.

Toshiko Akiyoshi (1929 -   )

Manchuria had yet to become a flashpoint for Japanese, Soviet, and Chinese armed forces when Toshiko Akiyoshi was born there, the child of Japanese parents. She began taking piano lessons at the age of seven. Her training was strictly classical; exposure to jazz was as remote a possibility as her geographical location would suggest. During the Chinese communist takeover of Manchuria in 1947, Akiyoshi's family returned to Japan, where she heard her first jazz record: Teddy Wilson's *Sweet Lorraine*. Hungry for more, she researched and analyzed Wilson and other masters' styles while working with a dance band at a US Army base in Tokyo. Practically all of jazz tradition was under her fingers in 1953, when Oscar Peterson heard her trio in a nightclub. On Peterson's recommendation, she recorded for Norman Granz, and secured a full scholarship at the Berklee School of Music.

After the completion of her Berklee studies in Boston (1959), Akiyoshi married saxophonist Charlie Mariano. In the '60s, she worked with Charles Mingus, co-led a quartet with her husband, and performed with her own trio. Clad in a traditional kimono, she rose above the racial and gender bigotry she encountered as an Asian woman playing jazz. Akiyoshi's second husband, saxophonist Lew Tabackin, whom she married in 1969, encouraged her interest in composition and orchestration. Ultimately, the pianist formed the big band that has been serving up her Ellingtonian scores, colorfully tinged with allusions to traditional Japanese music, since 1973. A successor of the fondly remembered Thad Jones-Mel Lewis band, the group appears regularly on Monday nights at Birdland.

Akiyoshi's devotion to writing has reduced her playing activities to a near stand-still. She robs us of a finely honed pianist in the Bud Powell tradition (*Akiyoshi at Maybeck* solo recital, Concord,1994). Always fussy about pianos ("Baldwins are independent, like cats; Steinways are more responsive, like dogs."), Akiyoshi draws out the full tonal majesty of a Yamaha S-400 B.

Renée Rosnes (1962 -   )

In 1994, a 32-year-old Renée Rosnes met her biological mother for the first time. The meeting connected some important dots concerning the pianist's Native American heritage. Shortly after the bittersweet reunion, her adoptive mother was diagnosed with terminal cancer. The effects of these traumas explain this artist's preoccupation with her ancestry, and her mounting interest in fusing jazz tradition with other musical cultures.

Born in Regina, Saskatchewan, Canada, Rosnes studied piano from the age of three and violin at six. Following continued study of the violin at the Royal Conservatory in Vancouver, she was introduced to jazz by her high school music teacher. She began playing piano gigs in Vancouver and in areas surrounding the campus of the University of Toronto, where she invested two years as a classical piano major. Gigs with visiting American soloists Dave Liebman and Joe Farrell spurred Rosnes to move to New York City in 1985. Recognition in the Apple was swift. By the time of her Blue Note recording debut as a leader (1988), she had toured and/or record-ed with Joe Henderson, Out of the Blue, Jon Faddis, J.J. Johnson, and Wayne Shorter. She has been in the company of boldface names ever since.

Rosnes makes a full disclosure of her assets in a growing discography. Moving closer and closer to the World Music rubric with her husband, drummer Billy Drummond, in tow, Rosnes is exploring the combination of several heterogeneous influences: the styles of Herbie Hancock and McCoy Tyner, and music from Native American, Far Eastern, African, and Brazilian sources. The result is a genuine synthesis. Rosnes is more successful than most at revealing how many seemingly disparate musical forms are; in essence, stone blocks from the same quarry.

Honorable Mention

Selecting the highest achievers among

the numberless participants in a musical

ethos a century old results in the unfortu-

nate collateral damage of an exclusionary

list. The following names were considered

for the main body of the book before

they were consigned to the status of hon-

orable mention.

Don Abney
Beegie Adair
Aloisio Aguiar
Joe Albany
Geri Allen
Helio Alves
Jimmy Amadie
Ben Aronov
Lynne Arriale
Joe Augustine
Bruce Barth
Richie Beirach
David Benoit
Ben Besiakov
Walter Bishop, Jr.
Eubie Blake
Claude Bolling
Beryl Booker
Evans Bradshaw
Alan Broadbent
Donald Brown
Rahn Burton
Michel Camilo

Ray Charles

Billy Childs

Mac Chrupcala

Sonny Clark

John Colianni

Johnny Costa

Rein DeGraff

Kenny Drew, Jr.

George Duke

Victor Feldman

Clare Fischer

Don Friedman

Dave Frishberg

Hal Galper

Jesse Green

Don Grolnick

Dave Grusin

Vince Guaraldi

Johnny Guarnieri

Bengt Hallberg

Harold Harris

Clyde Hart

Kevin Hays

Fred Hersch

Eddie Higgins

Jutta Hipp

Art Hodes

Bertha Hope

Elmo Hope

Stan Hope

Shirley Horn

Fred Hughes

Keith Ingham

Christian Jacob

Bob James

Jeff Jerolamon

Oliver Jones

Duke Jordan

Egil Kapstad

Dick Katz

Geoff Keezer

Roger Kellaway

Ray Kennedy

Kenny Kersey

Kenny Kirkland

Roy Kral

Diana Krall

Steve Kuhn

Billy Kyle

Ellis Larkins

Andy LaVerne

Hugh Lawson

Michael LeDonne

Michel Legrand

Brian Lemon

Mark Levine

Ramsey Lewis

Kirk Lightsey

Mike Longo

Jacques Loussier

Harold Mabern

Adam Makowicz

Pete Malinverni

Junior Mance

Michael "Dodo" Marmarosa

Ellis Marsalis

Dave Matthews

Jon Mayer

Lyle Mays	Adelaide Robbins	Ralph Sutton
Loonis McGlohon	Marcus Roberts	Cecil Taylor
Jim McNeely	Earl Rose	Richard Tee
Brad Mehldau	Ted Rosenthal	Jacky Terrasson
Mulgrew Miller	Gonzalo Rubalcaba	Sir Charles Thompson
Rob Mullins	Joe Sample	Ross Tompkins
Peter Nero	Stefan Scaggiari	Terry Trotter
Chris Neville	Hal Schaefer	Chucho Valdés
Herbie Nichols	Paul Schmeling	Mal Waldron
Walter Norris	Rob Schneiderman	George Wallington
Hod O'Brien	Hazel Scott	Bob Washhut
Johnny O'Neil	Stephen Scott	Randy Weston
Junko Onishi	Bernie Senensky	Gerald Wiggins
Makoto Ozone	Matthew Shipp	James Williams
Marty Paich	Don Shirley	Claude Williamson
Eddie Palmieri	Norman Simmons	Larry Willis
Horace Parlan	Cliff Smalls	Mike Wofford
Jeb Patton	Paul Smith	Joe Zawinul
Carl Perkins	Martial Solal	Denny Zeitlin
Michel Petrucciani	Jess Stacy	Bob Zurke
Terry Pollard	Lou Stein	
Freddie Redd	John Stetch	
Jack Reilly	Joe Sullivan	

About the Author

GENE RIZZO was born in 1940 in Tacony, a bustling northeast Philadelphia neighborhood dominated by smokestack industry. His father, a professional accordionist and an inveterate record collector, had little impact on his son's earliest career aspirations: Gene seemed set on becoming a writer/journalist. The years of subconscious exposure eventually kicked in, however, and after viewing a series of TV guest spots by Stan Getz, Billie Holiday, and Erroll Garner, the mid-teener firmly decided on the life of a musician. There was no turning back.

Gene's natural talent soon revealed itself on his grandparents' piano. Armed with some careful tutelage from his dad, he was already working professional gigs within a few months of his epiphany. By his early twenties, he was writing arrangements for singers and bands while studying piano and composition with Brazilian composer Burle Marx, a close associate of Heitor Villa-Lobos.

A musician of eclectic tastes, Gene has performed and written music in all styles and categories for more than forty years. Whether playing the harpsichord part in Vivaldi's *Gloria* with soprano Florence Quivar, accompanying singer Julius LaRosa, Fran Warren and film star Gloria de Haven, arranging for Lionel Hampton's band, or composing for the Baltimore Symphony and the New Zealand Viola Society, he applies himself with equal enthusiasm and skill.

Gene is currently Professor of Piano at Beaver College. He is also the author of the books *The Professional Solo Pianist: Techniques for the Self-Contained Performance of Jazz and Popular Music* and *Accompanying the Jazz/Pop Vocalist: A Practical Guide for Pianists*, both published by Hal Leonard Corporation. He still maintains his boyhood home in Philadelphia with his wife, Jeanne.